GW01375479

POETRY now

WE THINK THE WORLD OF ANIMALS

Edited by

Andrew Head

First published in Great Britain in 1998 by
POETRY NOW
1-2 Wainman Road, Woodston,
Peterborough, PE2 7BU
Telephone (01733) 230746
Fax (01733) 230751

All Rights Reserved

Copyright Contributors 1998

HB ISBN 1 86188 660 8
SB ISBN 1 86188 665 9

FOREWORD

The reason we write poetry (and almost all of us do) is because we want to communicate: an ideal; an idea; or a specific feeling. Poetry is as essential in communication, as a letter; a radio; a telephone, and the main criteria for selecting the poems in this anthology is very simple: they communicate.

We Think The World Of Animals is not only The World Society for the Protection of Animals' slogan, but is a sentiment that is practically written through the core of many of our supporters - like a stick of rock. This book is a testament to their feelings and observations about animals - whether they are describing their own pets - past and present - or animals in the wild that many of them may never even have seen in the flesh. Most poignant of all are the poems written about the animals that suffer at the hands of humans - animals that WSPA strives with considerable success to protect and save.

CONTENTS

Red, White And Blue	Valerie Jeffery	1
Hope	M Davies	2
The Truth About Man	Carla Marie Linnette	3
Four-Legged OAP	P Vance	4
Twinkie	Sue Bryce	4
For Eternity	M R Ogden	5
Bears	W M Francis	6
A New Life	Louise O'Hara	8
The Whales	Dixie Atkins	9
The Persistence Of Memory	D Koenigsberger	9
Obituary To The Fox	L Hammond Oberansky	10
My Dog Sophie	A J Drummond	11
Ursula's Ballroom Dancing Lesson	Jan Pearson	12
Why	Lesley Winton	13
A Picture Of Love	Emily Bell	14
Life In The Zoo	Chloe Stubbs	15
My Life Of Animal Friends	Karen Dennis	16
The Tiger	Judith Orr	17
Go Wild In The Country	H Philp	18
The Frog	Bridget Guyatt	18
Dog-Like Devotion	R G Page	19
The Shed Dogs	Pauline Bell	20
Silverback	M A Taylor	21
Sacrifice	Sheri-Lynne Johns	21
Is It Fair?	Gemma Macdonald	22
Sweet Dreams	Dawn Roper	22
Bas	Florence Doornbos-van Dijk	23
Little Bear	Lindi St James	24
Despair	Patricia Grant	25
Gone	Steve Moss	26
African Waterhole	Helen Dearing	27
Untitled	Hereward Pearce	28
My Friend	Natalie Marichal	28
Judgement	Adrian Cooper	29

Look Into My Eyes	Margaret Walker	30
Whale Dance	Jolene Neary	31
So Long As There Are Stars	Mary Cane	32
Untitled	Marnie Cude	32
The Bear's Question	A E Carr	33
Bumble Bee	Christine Dean	34
Manatees	Christopher Johnson	34
Who Cares For Bears?	Emily Rogers	35
African Elephant	Gillian Hulme	35
Nobby	Kaylie Day	36
The Dancing Bear	Madeline Pearson	36
I Am A Dancing Bear	Kate Dallison	37
Bosnian Bear	Dawn Faulkner	37
Untitled	Debra Barnett	38
Dancing Bear	Jenny Lim	39
Indignity	Caroline Tiller	39
The Wild Stallion	Edna M Russell	40
Watching A Toad . . .	Frances Wright	41
Fox-Hunting	Helen Cheetham	42
Another Day Gone	Mariam Uddin	42
Bear Of Burden, Bear Of Freedom	Judith M Cangiano	43
Blackest Clouds	Annette Marie Wilson	44
The Say Of The Jungle Brothers	Lawrence O Chongo	44
Life In The Jungle	Emily Cressey	45
A Wish For An Indian Elephant	Johannah Fawthrop	46
Pawprints	Jane Lawton	47
Untitled	R Postlethwaite	47
Cruelty To Animals	Jaymie Snowdon	48
Why?	Christine Peers	48
Imagine	Emily Sweet	49
Just	Heather Sutch	49
Misha (Bristol Zoo)	Peter Gillard	50
Aberration	Daf Richards	51
Now . . . And Then	Tricia Sturgeon	52
The Dog - Man's Best Friend!	Mary Asonga	53
The Myth Of The Green Bear	Berta R Freistadt	54

Gun Licence	Paddy Phillips	56
A Letter To Man: The Jungle Cry	Christine Khasina	57
A Tale For Three Bears	John Guy	58
The Animals And Mammals	E Browning	59
October Doom	Dorothea Carroll	60
A Buddhist Prayer	Anita Richards	61
The Fifth Commandment	Diana Oxford	62
Bear Cub	P Lopez	63
The Cry Of The Animals	Rosemarie Scott	64
A Happier Me	Lynn Greene	65
The Swan	Tony Vanner	66
Edward	Jayne-Louise Herbert	66
A Puppy Called Bengy	Nancy Bryant	67
Please	Clare Marshall	68
My Best Friend	Margaret A French	69
Come To Me Mother Seal	Linda Roth	70
Down By The Water-Hole	Katherine Delaney	71
Lady Blue	Tannsey Palmer	72
The Strays	Sonia Griffiths	73
Bears	Max Wakefield	73
Morning Sun	Rachel A Kruft	74
Mercy Rescue	Patricia E M Ayres	75
The Zebra Finch	Helen Wildbore	76
A Brown Bear In Albania	Elizabeth Wallace	77
Lest We Forget	Joan Ann Knipe	78
Thoughts	Lynn Gibbons	79
They Remember	Amanda Dinnivan	79
The Philosopher	Angela M Baber	80
Cargoes Of Innocence	Marian Allen	81
Trapped	Harold Brawn	82
Dog's Life	Diane Spreadborough	82
Abandoned	Lisa Bennett	83
Shall We Dance	Marguerite Piper	83
For Billie	Irene Reddish	84
All God's Creatures	Ruth Barclay Brook	85
Can't Bear To Look	Elaine Simmons	85
Grey Wolf	J M Park	86

The Cry	Lilian Gillard	87
Born To Be Free	Verity Holsgrove	88
Sanctuary	Chrissie	88
Animals Of The World	Marilyn Dunne	89
Beauty The Horse	Sheila Smith	90
Please Help Me	Maureen Russell	91
My Bears	Jan Clayton	91
The Tiger	Jessica-Ann Jenner	92
Brown Bear	Lydia Tweed	92
Just An Animal	D Sutton	93
Bears	Mary Welsh	93
The Awakening	Annette Lloyd	94
Bears	Wendy Marchant	94
Forgotten	Rachel Linden	95
Exploitation	Kit Jackson	96
The Lion	Jennifer Thomson	96
Every Day Could Be Its Last	Claire Capp	97
Swan	David Rigby	98
The Cat Cull	C Steele	99
Set Them Free	Ella Meah	100
Untitled	Francis Hodgkinson	100
Am I A Bear?	John Curtis Maddison	101
The Dancing Bear	Lindsay Maggs	102
An Appeal To God	Alistair Bain	102
Guilt	Gerry O'Neil	103
Animals On Film	Philip L Fletcher	104
Dancing Till Death	Helen Elizabeth Rawlinson	104
The Crocodile	Carol Lycett	105
Freedom	Jim Deakin	105
Animal Poem	Andrea Sidney	106
Protect Our Animals	Kenneth J Ody	106
Mercy On Montserrat	Marjorie Houston	107
Brown Eyes	Carol Deakin	108
Lynx In The Snow	Marie Hurlston	109
Fighting Bear	Lyn Errington	110
When The Cruelty Stops	P E Tidswell	110
Chimp	Tania Sutlieff	111

Sunday Morning . . .	David Hardy	112
The Prisoner	Rachel Martin	113
The Bear's Prayer	Jenny Prin	114
So Young	Carol Bones	114
The Vixen	Lynne Chitty	115
Innocent Victim	Helen Perry	116
Untitled	C P Goodwin	117
Animals	Veronica Searle	117

RED, WHITE AND BLUE

White expanse of ice,
Blue expanse of sky,
Mothers with new babies,
Soon about to die.

We fought so hard to save them,
In the years gone by,
Women favoured fur coats,
The reason they would die.

Once again their lives at risk,
They cannot understand,
Why these towering people,
Have bats and guns in hand.

On the far side of the world,
Is the aphrodisiac trade,
And for seals' body parts,
Much money will be paid.

And so once more the upturned eyes
Bewildered, frightened, pleading,
Are bashed and battered on red ice,
In pools of blood lie bleeding.

What gives us the right to act,
In such a brutal way?
To use, abuse whatever's there.
Because it has no say!

These gentle, soft-eyed creatures,
May not have a choice,
But *we* can be their champions,
We *must* be their voice.

Valerie Jeffery

HOPE

Animals are such a comfort
They give so much joy
Yet they undergo so much suffering
Only some get joy.
Some people love to hurt them
And inflict sorrow and pain
God help stop this cruelty
And let them live again.

The world is full of wonder
The sun is shining bright
The sea is calm but rugged
And fish are swimming about.
The boat is floating slowly
As peace surrounds the earth
Tranquillity and wonder
Fills the universe
The birds are nesting
The animals having their young
Pray all people come together
And unite as one.

Animals and children
Need tender love and care
Not hurt and abandonment
Only love beyond compare
Why do grown-ups
Abuse and hurt them
And neglect their daily needs
When they give such love and pleasure
And feed our many needs.

Bears and cubs are playing
What a wonderful sight
No dangers are looming
Only contentment and flight
Such fun they are having
Adventures galore
Each day they are learning
That little bit more.

M Davies

THE TRUTH ABOUT MAN

Late at night is when I shed my tears, I picture my whole life, hopes and fears.
You see I feel my heart torn in two, when I see our animals suffer and don't know what to do.
Mankind is no more than cruel, too obsessed with power and rule.
When I see dolphins panic and cry, drowning in drift nets waiting to die,
A feeling enters me, one I can't explain I feel much regret, hate and pain
Gorillas' hands taken away, never again to feel the light of day.
Tigers' penises cut off with knives when they should have been used to create new lives.
Orphaned babies wander the land because their mothers were killed by the human hand.
Live baby calves on the roads for hours, when they should be in fields enjoying the flowers.
Elephants' only crime is their tusks so white, poachers come and hack at night.
Baby seals' heads bashed in. Why? because they have such beautiful skin.
Mankind! What an ironic word to give! When *kind man* cruelly kills all creatures that live.

Carla Marie Linnette

Four-Legged OAP

My little dog is getting old,
her puppy days long gone,
her once black face has now turned grey,
as the years roll steadily on.

She doesn't seem to walk as far,
I think her legs are sore,
she doesn't want to play as much
the way she did before.

She's happy just to be with me,
and sleep upon the chair,
Just waking up now and then,
to make sure I am there.

Her food needs to be soft now,
her teeth aren't very good,
and when I have to bathe her,
she's just not in the mood.

But even though she's getting old,
she's still my greatest pleasure,
and every day I have with her,
is another memory to treasure.

P Vance

Twinkie

A little bear named Twinkie
Sat lonely in a zoo,
He had no friends to play with,
And nothing much to do.

The owner never visited,
Nor were there passers-by,
He very rarely had a meal,
And a tear formed in his eye.

But then a wondrous thing did happen,
On a very special day,
Some kindly people rescued him,
From the WSPA.

Now he's a field to run in,
And a lake in which to swim,
If only it could happen to all bears,
So glad it happened to him.

Sue Bryce

For Eternity

The seas which once were clear and blue are now a dirty grey.
I'm told it is the effluence which people flush away.
The fishes, lobsters and crabs galore
Are looking for a cleaner shore.
The sea birds too have had their fill
Of oil slicks that clog their bills,
Sometimes they cannot fly
Eventually they often die.

Are we to share in this disgrace?
The problem stems from the human race
We say we love all living things, can this really be true?
For if we did, I'm sure we would see the harm we all do.
Before we litter the streams, sea and sand,
Let's try to make this a better land,
A place where animals large and small,
Fishes, insects and birds galore
Can live together along our shores.
Let us try and make our world a better place to be,
Not just for a few weeks or years, but for eternity.

M R Ogden

BEARS

They said write something - about the bear
but *they* are impotent, those who'd hear.

But those whose atrocities of pain inflict
Own no perception or intellect
Only appetites of gaping horrors
Grinning perversions
 - steel studded collars.

They made me ashamed
I'm one of them
Ashamed of my species,
So called human.

No wonder those magnificent mobile towers
Have teeth and claws, great defensive powers.
He knew the filth strutting upright on two.
He knew the stench of human brew.

I cry inside but it helps them not
I rant and rage because of their lot.

My anger indulged,
frustration sated.
What good does it do
those horribly baited.

No words of mine can decently right
the pain and suffering, their helpless plight.
Respect and humility cannot counter the evil.
Hollow oaths and prose to counter the devil?!

I can pray, I can shout and fret from afar
Write letters and storm the fates as they are,
But I know it continues, the pulling of claws,
The yanking of teeth and collars of sores.
No deadening ether, just realised fear.
Their cubs are too the subject of abject despair
The setting of dogs with foaming teeth
While poor bleeding giants in agonised grief
Have no chance, no defence.
No mercy from them, the disgusting monsters
Who call themselves men.

And yes, I am guilty, I am one
If I sit back and say there is none,
None action. None care.
None feeling. Nowhere,

But I *am* involved. I am to blame
I'm here and alive, yes, just the same
I'm human - human?
Yes, just the same
Do nothing at all?
Then I *am* to blame.

One prayer then in hope so weak,
A whispered murmur not daring to speak

Let it be over
Let it be done
Slip away to an Eden
where healing streams run
'Mid honey and grass, trees
in the shade
I will dream them a peace of oblivion made.

They did not ask to be
You gave them little choice
So perhaps my busy tongue
Could be their hopeless voice.

But who sits by
This peaceful stream
Musing o'er this cosy dream
'Tis not the wretched bears for sure.
'Tis only I indulged once more.

W M Francis

A NEW LIFE

'Clip, clop,' she said, sarcastically
As my pace slowed
Quite drastically.
The moon hung low
Reminding me
That I was far from dignity.
The whip struck hard
And stung my skin
And devils' hands and heels dug in.
For hours and hours we wend our way
And nothing that my wounds could say
Would stop her even though her own
Legs were by far the better bet.

In honesty, when I look back
And try to think what made her bad
I cannot
For the warmth that's shown
Now by new friends
Has made a home.
And even when my stomach churns
(From satisfaction, not from worms),
I think of all the better things
A rescue and some love can bring.

Louise O'Hara

THE WHALES

Do you see the whales?
Diving, drifting, gliding,
                lazy on the slow sea sliding.
Hiding silent in the undefined deep,
                where drowned men sleep.
Upsweep of two-pronged tail
                lets fall a glistening silvered trail.
Whale blows and spouts and spumes
                until the sea with fury fumes.
Plumes of jagged water slashing;
                monstrous body thrashing,
Crashing beneath the harpoon sting.
                Swift spreading crimson ring.
Nothing. Nothing.
Will our children see the whales?

Dixie Atkins

THE PERSISTENCE OF MEMORY

This is a day of fantastical images,
of bears doing solemn dances in the rain,
of owls turned cat in tense anticipation;
these sentinels watch us. Their contemplation
brings to mind many things long buried
in boots and trunks hidden in our attics;
these rising to the surface thoughts, now hurried,
were long ago things once, dormant and static.
Amid this picture puzzle from our past,
from rainy days on trains when we were small,
we see and smell and taste them, hold them all,
and wonder whether now we know the truth.
Of how to weigh and whether we can solve
impressions of the past that don't dissolve.

D Koenigsberger

OBITUARY TO THE FOX

I am cold, I am hungry, with an aching soul
In fear of my life, for I am used as a tool;
To be chased across meadows and fields I have loved,
Where in spring I have drifted through poppies and maize
And cherished the sun of those warm, sacred days:
I've rolled in the dewy grass and lived off the land.
Kept mice from the farms and rats from infesting their barns.

Many of my friends have been driven to rural suburbs and towns:
If only I had known the right direction to take.
For I would not now be hearing the hounds
Perhaps food would have been more readily prepared for I have heard
That many town folk left something for us outside their doors.

For me it is too late to muse,
My body throbs as though to burst
And such a burning covers my paws.
This cannot last any longer
The chase is near the end.
My body will become no stronger,
My time is near the end,
The hounds draw closer.

Their savage guard rides on.
When my blood is spilt, he feels that he will have won:
But yet, the savage redcoat guard,
Their lives, as yet, not done,
But in their doing, they will be undone.

All creatures great and small
Are created by the Lord,
And wrong doings, by Him are stored,
In their doing they will be undone.

L Hammond Oberansky

MY DOG SOPHIE

My Sophie understands me,
She knows just what I mean
When I ask her questions
About places she has been.
'How could you get so muddy?'
She's very swift to tell,
'I've been swimming in the river,'
She answers with her smell!

My Sophie tries to teach me
To follow in her ways
By patiently repeating
The important things she says.
She has her ways of stating
'It's time for me to go'
I'm not sure what her barking means
(It's better I don't know!)

My Sophie likes to watch me
With eyes that rarely blink
They're trying to unravel
The eccentric way I think.
'When rabbits are out running
Why does he leave so late?
Yet when they're in their burrows
He's first to reach the gate.'

I know my Sophie loves me
How else can one explain
Her standing by a numskull
To whom nothing is quite plain
She gives me reassurance
Head nestling on my knee
She knows I'm not too clever
So loves me tenderly.

A J Drummond

URSULA'S BALLROOM DANCING LESSON

Intro:
    I'll dance for you
    because you tug at my face
    with your ropes

    I'll hop and I'll shamble
    because I am shackled

    You'll laugh at my antics
    the corners of your mouth tugged
    towards your eyes

    You'll clap
    and you'll cackle
    because you are tethered

Lesson:
    Cut my rough rope

    I'll bite through your bonds.

Finale: The Waltz (*Ursula leads*)
Look at me
    One two three
Hold out your hands
    two three
Move with me
    one two three
    one two three
Now we are one
    two three
Now you are free
    two three
Now I am me
    two three
Now
    we can dance

Jan Pearson

Why

Your gentleness, your compassion, your trust
Why is such pain
inflicted upon you?
Your intelligence, your loyalty, your superiority
we don't deserve you.

The world would be devoid of meaning
if you didn't exist.
We can learn so much from you
Why are we so naive
so callous?

Your splendour knows no bounds
yet look what we can reduce you to.
You are completely at our mercy
and we abuse you.

Why?
Why? Why? Why?
You have a right to life
perhaps more so than us.
If we destroy you, we destroy ourselves.

When will the human race learn,
What goes around comes around?
Your world is our world.
Pain inflicted on you
is inflicted on ourselves.

Lesley Winton

A PICTURE OF LOVE

There in the corner,
Lies ragged sheets, dirty and strewn,
Under the dark table, scratched and worn.
But, something beautiful is there,
Ten tiny pups!
Their mother, proud and protective,
Like a hawk guarding its nest,
Curled round the puppies,
Caring and loving.
The puppies, one day old,
Are squirming around their mum.
Eyes are tightly shut,
Dreaming, smiling eyes.
Their sleek coats are as black as coal,
And their fronts are dipped in white.
One is all white, a coat of silver,
Bossing the others around.
Trying to get the most of the creamy milk.
They squawk like seagulls,
Sharp but quiet,
A beautiful song,
The song of their future . . .
Their tiny pink noses,
Damp and soft,
Like a stick of pink candyfloss,
Delicate and dreamy.
Their rough, red paws,
Feeble and uncoordinated,
Are a beautiful contrast to their delicate noses.
Stiff and tiny,
Thin and strong,

The tails stand upright,
Like a pole without a flag,
They follow their heavy, soft bodies,
Absentmindedly.
A picture of care, tenderness and warmth,
A picture of love.

Emily Bell

LIFE IN THE ZOO

Look at that bear;
Isn't he tough,
I've heard that phrase
often enough.
It's way past feeding time;
have they forgotten?
I'd eat yesterday's food if
it hadn't gone rotten.
Oh look people say he's
scratching his head;
and he's sitting in a pit or
is that his bed?
Here comes the zoo keeper,
about time too.
That's just one disadvantage
of living in a zoo.
It's getting dark now
so I sprawl out on the floor,
There's still so many people;
how many more?
So many people
why can't they see;
I don't want to be here;
I want to be free.

Chloe Stubbs

MY LIFE OF ANIMAL FRIENDS

As far back as I can remember
We had a dog called Amanda,
She behaved badly - was rather a tyke!
Me, I'm afraid she did not like
I'm never sure if she grew old
Don't think I was ever told.

Later there was Karl - he caught distemper
Gentle and kind, showed no temper
A lovely dog, Mum nursed back to health
To be rewarded, but not with wealth
But a grateful, loyal friend
Until a sad day that became his end

Chippy, the budgie, I had to call my own
The cage tipped over, away he had flown
Timothy the tortoise and several fish
A grand assortment, all you could wish!

Along came Ricky from a rescue home
he was a boxer, who loved his bone
Ricky led Mum a fine old dance
Over a six foot fence he would prance
Sadly his life came to an end
Goodbye to yet another friend!

When I got married we had a cat,
Her name was Brandy - snoozed on the mat,
For seventeen years, our life-long friend
Until, sadly, another pet's life's end.

We then had Holly, a nervous pup
Who would drink if she could from your cup
Before we knew it, she was fourteen years old
Her legs giving way - we didn't have to be told
Another pet's life passed yet again
The decision was hard to ease the pain.

So now we have two lovely cats
Who love to be fussed with pats
One named Bonny, the other, Amber
Children grown up - they're mine to pamper
I'm sure we'll have them for years to come
Living in luxury - lucky for some!

Karen Dennis

THE TIGER

I wake up to another day
And ponder on what I shall have,
For some unlucky animal
It is going to be the end of their day.

As I walk through the trees,
My eye catches a movement,
I turn round, and there it is,
My first meal of the day.

It has not seen me yet,
As I stalk it, I see it looking at me,
It breaks into a run, I pursue,
I gradually gain on it and then . . .

It vanishes, nowhere to be seen.
I look around, conscious of it
looking at me,
I hear a rustle, I turn round and
there it is.

I break into a run, it does too,
I'm nearly there, just a few strides more,
I pounce, and I catch it,
It is the end of its day.

Judith Orr (12)

GO WILD IN THE COUNTRY

Out in the meadow,
Black and white cows,
Happily grazing,
The lambs are a-leaping,
Horses standing in their paddocks,
Down on the farm, waddling ducks,
Swimming on the pond,
Going round and round,
Muddy pigs in their sties,
Birds flying high in the sky,
Building nests to have their young,
Bumble bees - mind you don't get stung,
Foxes hunting on the ground,
Bunnies don't make a sound,
In the fields so green,
Yet some of nature goes unseen,
Insects the eye can't see,
Squirrels clambering in the trees,
Nature so wild and free,
All this for you and me.

H Philp

THE FROG

At first we see the egg in spawn
In the pond beside the lawn,
Into a tadpole then he'll hatch.
While our cat dips paw to catch.

When one week old, small gills appear,
But at three weeks these disappear,
And when the tadpole's six weeks old
We see hind legs appear so bold.

When he's reached his eleventh week
In the pond you'll see a freak,
With tail and all his four legs now,
Soon to the world he'll make his bow.

At the age of fourteen weeks
The cat with eagerness now seeks -
Prowling around the pond with glee
The full-grown frog to eat for tea.

Bridget Guyatt

DOG-LIKE DEVOTION

Fond memories still prevail
    Of four legs and a tail
That used to follow me around
    Or almost floor me with a welcoming bound.
She loved to walk me round where water is about
    So she could dive and swim and try it out.

Of course she often got me soaking wet
    And quite as damp as became my pet
Yet she had so many delightful tricks
    She gave me some encouraging licks
That I was always bound
    To have her around.

Now she has moved on to higher things
    And perhaps is walking around with kings
Perhaps she will come across some angelic lake
    Where she'll swim around for goodness sake
I am sure she'll be giving her devotion
    To some saintly person.

R G Page

THE SHED DOGS

We are the shed dogs
Wary at dawn,
Alone at our station
Ready to warn.
Grimily coated
Eyes forlorn,
Guarding the junk and dustbins.

We are the shed dogs
As the moon beams
We jump and we run
In brief dreams.
Feel the rough tussocks
Under our feet,
Swim in imaginary streams.

But, we are the shed dogs
With nerves on taut strings,
We share our dark shed
With old tyres and things.
On nights when the raging
Rainstorm brings
Thunderous echoes of fear,
Remember the shed dogs
Remember us, do,
Remember a prayer . . .
Or a tear.

Pauline Bell

SILVERBACK

A powerful black figure is he
Head of a hairy family.
To be found in forests of Zaire
The likes of which, not known here.

A silverback gorilla
Notably, a most intelligent fella.
His habitat uprooted by man
Food now scarce for the little one.

Ensnared in painfully devised traps
Defencelessly gunned down, perhaps!
More than a thought to our planet friend
Before he reaches an untimely end.

M A Taylor

SACRIFICE

Elephants are killed for their ivory tusks
Which are carved to make ornaments.
Rhinos are shot or electrocuted for their horns
Which are used to make special dagger handles.
Tigers are killed for their warm, coloured coats
Which are made into extravagant coats.
None of these are needed for our survival
but are crucial for theirs. So why not . . .
Sacrifice your ivory ornaments instead of
sacrificing an entire species of elephant,
Sacrifice your special dagger handle instead of
sacrificing an entire species of rhino.
Sacrifice your extravagant fur coat instead of
sacrificing an entire species of tiger.

Sheri-Lynne Johns (15)

IS IT FAIR?

Is it fair that animals
are mistreated?
Sanctuaries keep trying
but so far have been
defeated.
Why are they treated
differently to the human race?
The way that they are
treated is really a
disgrace.
Maybe in a couple of
years,
Care will break
through.
But until then the only
person that can help
Is you!

Gemma Macdonald (11)

SWEET DREAMS

I sit at night
while you sleep,
Licking my paws
Brushing your feet
I sit and stare
at your restful eyes,
Patiently waiting
as morning grows nigh
I sit and watch your dreams disappear.
As the sunlight awakes
My mistress dear.

Dawn Roper

BAS

Or Bas,
so brave, so watchful.
So frail, so happy,
and suddenly you have gone,
you are not here any more with us.
It all went so fast,
we cannot believe it.
The *why* written in such large letters.
'Cause you are our little Bas, our Great Dane,
Always you wanted to be so close with us,
and the best of all, sitting on our laps,
the place you were a lot of the time.
In our hearts you will live forever,
We can, will never forget you.
The sadness is great, the tears flow,
Our hearts cry,
'cause Bas,
We cannot live without you.
You are so special, unique,
our Bassele Baby.
Why, oh *why?*
Puck is looking for you, he is so sad.
He is crying and asking 'Where is my brother?'
We cannot tell him
Basseman, thank you for all you have given us,
you will always be with us.

Florence Doornbos-van Dijk

LITTLE BEAR

Little bear
in a cage
Not much older
than my daughter's age
Torn from your mother
in the wild
You are but a tiny,
frightened child.

Little bear
all alone
You should not be
this far from home
Scared and bewildered
you cannot understand
The inhumanity
of mankind.

Little bear
so frightened now
You try and protect yourself
with a tiny growl
For they have taken the teeth
from your baby cub mouth
And pulled out the claws
from your tiny paws
And soon you will learn of
more fear and pain
As they set the dogs on you
again . . . and again.

Little bear lies softly now
No more the tiny, baby growl
There is only blood
and a terrified stare
And more pain
than any human could bear.

Little bear
you close your eyes
And remember blue rivers
and sunny skies
The feel of your mother
and the smell of the air
And you wish more than anything
you could be there.

Be brave, little bear
For we love you dearly
And we are fighting
to set you free
And to take you to the safety
at the Sanctuary
And for all the other bears
both large and small
Libearty is fighting
to save you all
And to break the bars
of every cage
To stop this inhumane
outrage.

Lindi St James

DESPAIR

'A bear!'
'Where?'
'Over there,
Basking in the sun.'

But a tug at the rope
Means there's no hope
As dancing is no fun.

Patricia Grant

GONE

I knew this friendly Crowther Bear
on the Atlas Mountain range;
He used to tell me stories
So fantastical and strange

He liked to play and roll about
He was such a happy chap,
But most of all, he liked to growl
Before he had his nap.

Crowther was a lonesome bear
But soon became my chum,
We'd often have a picnic,
And he always would be mum.

He listened so intensely
As I told him what I'd seen
Of greed, and pain and hunger
And of murder in between

One day we played his favourite game
And Crowther went to ground
I searched for him for days and nights
But never heard a sound

Perhaps my loyal friend just got bored,
But I seeked until I cried,
And I really miss old Crowther
Since the day he went to hide.

Steve Moss

AFRICAN WATERHOLE

Dusk,
A glittered orange sky,
With a cricket-chorus melody
Slowly,
The animals drink;

> Impalas jump friskily,
> Warthogs raise aerieled tails,
> Elephants pull up wrinkly trousers,
> Giraffes swoop elegant necks.

And among the crowd merge the zebras' stripes

Commotion begins,
As the predators arrive.
Docile drinkers scatter as;

> Jackals dart cunningly,
> Wild dogs barking breaks the still,
> While hyenas' cackle echo on.

But now all clear the water's edge,
Golden locks catch the sun,
Teeth glimmer with menace,
Thunderous paws leave hollow craters.

All watch,
Silently
As the mighty one drinks.
All breaths
Are bated.

Helen Dearing

UNTITLED

What to save today?
Tiger, bears, dogs, donkeys,
All need our help
Rotting in Taiwan, chained in Turkey,
Mauled in Pakistan, stabbed in Spain
The pain, the pain, the pain

What to save today?
Cats, gorillas, parrots, cows,
Who will hear our plea,
Angry in Mayfair, disgusted in Croydon
Heartbroken in Blackburn, distraught in Teesside
The pain, the pain, the pain

What to save today?
Torture in Cuba caused tears in Teesside
But never enough to help
Cheques, sponsored walks
Charity giving, corporate donations
It's always the same, the pain, the pain, the pain.

Hereward Pearce

MY FRIEND

My old friend elephant
With your big floppy ears
but please beware my old
friend as your life lives in fear.

Your tusks are sold for money
Your body left to rot
Please beware my old friend
as I love you a lot.

Natalie Marichal (13)

JUDGEMENT

If I were you (thank God I'm not!) but if I was
The world would have an extra and a nasty human being because
You have abandoned love. The sickening pride that swamps your brain
Dictates a very selfish pleasure; the reason why you treat my strain
Like furniture, machines and trash. Unless of course we count as cash,
Then welfare is a must.

Rosettes and cups from shows and trials -
You cut a dash! And I tried hard to please each time
We went into the ring. The adulation, clapping, your superior smiles
Which lasted till the day I passed my peak and winning prime.
You kicked me! Fireside and basket changed to draughty shed
                                                        and straw.
The grooming stopped. Two minutes exercise to see the light of day;
Hours of solitude, my cry ignored; old crusts shoved underneath
                                                        the door
As if I was a useless thing. A time approached to lay
And wait. Release from your neglect and curses; weakness,
                                                    thirst and pain.
You drank indoors, the merry life, while I slid down to death; insane.

When your turn comes how will you answer for your chosen course?
Even the humble sparrow's fall my higher Master can detect.
He suffered violence from your species, cruelty; loss of all respect;
The self-same evils you embrace and soon must bear eternal in remorse.
So much degraded wealth and power wholly forced to leave behind.
Nothing carried over: except the slow parade of victims through
                                                       your mind.

Adrian Cooper

LOOK INTO MY EYES
(The silent cry of a dancing bear)

Another minute,
Another hour,
Another day,
Another face dismisses coins from his pocket,
To become witness to my dance.

People watch on,
Their ignorant smiles widen,
As they become transfixed on this pointless spectacle.

My eyes appeal to my master,
Begging for mercy,
But he cannot hear my silent cries,
And will not look into my eyes.

The crowd applauds,
At the movement of my legs,
They choose not to see,
The movement of the chain which tugs at my flesh.

And I can see the innocence,
In the eyes of a child before me,
But no one will see the innocence,
In mine.

I want them to look into my eyes,
To witness my pain,
Please look into these eyes,
Which once shot fear into the heart of every man,
But now glaze over with fear,
And reflect an image of lost dignity.

Look into my eyes,
Look into my eyes,
See what I see,
Hear what I hear,
Feel what I feel.

But I am alone,
And fade into insignificance,
As the faces around me,
Move further and further into the crowd.

Margaret Walker

WHALE DANCE

The sun is smiling down on the ocean yet again.
The shallows of bright light shine so smoothly on the sea's surface.
The whale pack stirs, gently, the graceful creatures full of beauty
and integrity raise their heads.
They begin to dive in small slow movements at first, each one waiting
for the other to begin their ritual of swimming techniques.
The leader is the oldest and the wisest of them all.
His pale grey skin, grazed from many battles proves that he does not
begin or even attempt the idea of inviting danger.
The youngest is filled with energy.
His eyes smile like that of a field of sunflowers, his skin so shiny, so
shiny that it looks like a sheet of glass held in the sun's rays.
The sun has now hidden itself beneath a gathering of dark cloud.
Rain has broken splashing down on the ocean like there's no tomorrow.
The youngest whale starts to swim around in circles, diving in
high motions.
The rain does not bother him, for he loves the very presence of it.
Soon the pack are all behind him, following in his every stride, sharing
the fun of the 'Whale Dance'.
It is one truly stunning scene, a scene that could only ever be
lived once.
The true beauty of this nature is not for words to explain, only sound
and vision may capture these moments.
The ocean is heaven's gate. If we had more harmony than power, then
maybe we could find the key.

Jolene Neary

SO LONG AS THERE ARE STARS

The night was once so full of stars
And life was free and sweet;
A cub no more he knew but bars,
Rough voices, pain and heat . . .

They forced him every day to stand
On sore back feet and - and sway
To drum and rattle's tuneless band
And always to obey . . .

His tender nose was ringed and bound
And jerked by leather thong;
Amid the jeers of those around
He tried to prance along . . .

Until, as time went dragging by,
His movement slowed with age;
Regardless of his whimpering cry
They left him in his cage . . .

But someone came when life seemed gone
And promised Sanctuary;
His cage now open to the stars
The dancing bear was free!

Mary Cane

UNTITLED

I get the feeling they just don't care
About this poor and hungry bear

Just look at the filth around this place
And what's been done to scar my face.

Someday I hope someone will set me free
All I want now is *Libearty!*

Marnie Cude

THE BEAR'S QUESTION

Tell me men what have I done?
Why must you exploit my body so?
I wish to roam and live as one.
My huge limbs and head hang low.

I cannot help the way I was born,
And do not wish my parts all torn,
The pain's enough for a bear to bear.
All I know is your cruel fear,
So tell me men what have I done?
Why do you exploit my body so?
I wish to roam and live as one.
My huge limbs and head hang low.

I pace up and down on a chain of steel,
And you don't know of the pain I feel,
I wish I could speak and tell my tale,
But I can't I'm imprisoned to a wooden pale,
Please for the sake of all animal-kind,
Not just for me but all who are blind.

Tell me men what have I done?
To warrant you to exploit my body so?
I wish to roam and live as one,
But my huge limbs and head hang low,
And still the blood from scars doth flow.

The mental strain is so much I know,
Let me live as I was supposed to be,
Happy and contented free so free,
But you still exploit my body so,
And still my huge limbs and head hang low.

One day my huge head will be held up high,
On that day I'll look toward the sky,
And wonder men, why, oh why, oh why?

A E Carr

BUMBLE BEE

A wide windowsill
Where tall hollyhocks lean outside
And tap the window, swaying
Big round faces in the wind.
A bee lies dead on the white brick
Upon his back,
Soft as round brown fur
And powder white rump
Unblemished.
Fine transparent wings
With tracery like stained glass
Glowing with leaf-brown light.
His stiff legs, touched with down,
Seized sadly beneath his chin
In a last fierce holding of life.
Antennae, bent like a frame
Around the great dragon's eyes
Which shone like polished ovals
In the black face.

Christine Dean

MANATEES

Dogs with flippers in the sea
there're Mr and Mrs Manatee
swimming in a sea of blue
with the little babies too.
But out great big motor boats with sails
chop our poor old friends' small tails
so don't kill our nice dogs with flippers
with our huge big water skippers.

Christopher Johnson (9)

WHO CARES FOR BEARS?

They're big and fluffy they roam all around,
They play with each other they also pound,
All over the world they have dancing bears,
    Who cares?
        We do!

Black Cloud was a victim like lots of others,
They get taken so young away from their mothers.
People watch the dogs tear them apart,
    Who cares?
        We do!

Why do people do it for fun?
Why can't you just let them run?
Away from horror!
Away from attack!
Why can't you just get off their backs?
    Who cares?
        We care!

Emily Rogers (11)

AFRICAN ELEPHANT

Alone, alone in the sweltering sun,
Water a distant memory.
This dead land,
Lush green trees which once were seen
Now stripped bare
By the others who have been.
Now the distressing sound which haunts me
Is above in the clouds,
The pitiful end is drawing in,
Is here - once man has killed me
For his selfish means.

Gillian Hulme (15)

NOBBY
(1.12.1977- 24.11.1995)

Nobbs, Nobby Nobbykins
In life and sadly in death
My heart he always wins
And now he lies asleep beneath
My window. I cannot forget
That in life and even at the end
He remained my most devoted friend
And so it is with deep regret
I bid farewell, to one who gave his all
Who loyally responded to my every call
Nobbykins, Nobby, Nobbs
You have left a heart that sobs
But I will remember you always
Throughout the years and the long days
Without you it is lonely and so very flat
But please, rest in peace my beloved cat.

Kaylie Day

THE DANCING BEAR

He stood there fettered by a chain
I saw his eyes, I felt his pain
The music played, he tried to jig
Not very graceful, he's so big.
his captor hit him with a rod
and shouted 'I said dance not plod'
This lovely creature seemed in a trance
a big brown bear that was made to dance.
I cried out, 'This was not meant to be,
undo the chain and set him *free*.

Madeline Pearson

I Am A Dancing Bear

Come and watch me dance for you.
I can twist and turn like a ballerina
I am as elegant as a swan
I am as beautiful as a bird
I don't make mistakes,
I daren't make mistakes
If I make a mistake I am beaten black and blue.
I hate my life travelling around like a train,
Dancing, getting beaten every night.
I wish I could have got away from that big fat man
Who killed my mum.
I can still remember cuddling up to her,
I cried every day and night for weeks.
Six years later I can still see my brother playing in the pond.
I will escape out of this slum one day

One day soon.

Kate Dallison (15)

Bosnian Bear

Oh Bosnian bear, in a country war-torn,
Never knowing any different, since the day you were born,
Bullets and gun-shots are the sounds you have grown to hear,
Surrounding your small cage of fear,
They came to your aid, 'those men in green'
And took you to things you had never seen,
You can now swim in a river, and climb a tree,
And know at last, what it is like, to feel free,
So, be safe, and be happy, Bosnian bear,
And may you live life to the full,
Rest assured 'Humans do care!'

Dawn Faulkner

UNTITLED

A dark figure in the night
Seen only by the moon so bright
A graceful head turns to the left, then to the right.

Soon the nights ends and the sky turns blue
No longer is it quiet, there's things to do
Her eyes have a meaning of the things to come
The meaning of the tall man who carries a gun
Then the trees rustle and the lion cries
The whole jungle shrivels and dies
He's out for pleasure and out for an aim
He'll get no Cup or any fame
The animals know he's there
They will move away, they have to care

The magnificent feline, the puma
Knows she can no longer run
Her time is here to give birth
She stops and lies down from the blazing sun.
But two steps away is the hunter and his gun
He's sees his kill and knows there'll be no trouble
She looks into his eyes begging for mercy
But his eyes are cold and he's no thought
She's in pain from the cubs to be born
She tries to move and painfully cries
And two eyes close as she slowly dies.

Debra Barnett

DANCING BEAR

A bear I am
A bear you may not be
But you and I
are of the same family.

You can, you did.
You prayed for me.
I so long to be free.

Thank you for
Praying for me.

Soon, very soon,
I, too will be
Dancing free.

*(In God I trust; I will not be afraid.
What can man do to me?' Psalm 56:11)*

Jenny Lim

INDIGNITY

What an unnatural sight
Made to perform against his will
No chance to rest or drink
Dancing means hurt; a hard-learned skill
Will no-one help him in his plight?

He does not deserve such pain
A pseudo-bear in a bearskin
Ill-treatment and heat make him weak
A short life apart from his kin
Pleasure solely for man's gain.

Caroline Tiller

THE WILD STALLION

His noble head held high
His silhouette against the sky
Showing the strength of powerful limbs
Like a statue he stands.

He fought to lead and won
A compelling urge driving him on
Savage and cruel is his punishment
Supremacy is his.

On the hill now he stands
The herd below waiting command
His sense will lead them, his strength protect
Defending with his life.

Only man need he fear
Scenting rank smell when he's near
Urging, sending the herd into flight
Across the dusty plains.

Anger spurring him on
Until energy spent and danger is gone
And the beat of hooves thunder no more
Proud in his triumph.

Long vigil now he keeps
While the herd drop their heads to sleep
They will be safe 'neath his watchful eye
His power now complete.

Edna M Russell

WATCHING A TOAD...

What an excellent creature is the toad
A prehistoric charm
Yet he moves in the glistening lily pool
With a perfect grace and calm

What practical features has the toad
So logically he's arranged
With eyes situate at the top of his head
Clever, rather than strange

An accomplished fine fellow, that's the toad
With both land and water a bond;
Eyes sleepily blinking a signal
To some outpost across the pond.

A much-maligned fellow is the toad
'So ugly' some say, without care.
He's chanting a song, perhaps to his mate,
Would *she* not think he is fair?

A leisurely gentleman is the toad
Centuries-wise is his face
Sunning his speckles, taking his time
What sense is the fast human pace?

A pleasure I find in watching the toad
His throat gently beats on the water
As he who has two worlds looks up at me,
I wonder . . . is that - silent laughter?

Frances Wright

Fox-Hunting

Run, run, as fast as you can
try but don't succeed
for all your fears come behind you
snapping at their feed

The pain begins
and then you fall
you look around
then start to crawl
but it's no good
for here they come
to tear you limb from limb

So run, run, as fast as you can
try but won't succeed
for all your fears come behind you
so run in desperate need.

Helen Cheetham

Another Day Gone

Through the day
These men stay far away
But during the night
That they all put up the fight.

And behind the bushes
A shadowy figure rushes
The trigger is pulled
The whole vision is dulled.

The silence is broken
And the whole of nature is woken
Another species gone
Now there is none.

Mariam Uddin

BEAR OF BURDEN, BEAR OF FREEDOM

I will break your chains
I will heal your wounds
I will make you forget the torture of years gone by.
I will give you shelter
I will give you food and water . . .

But I cannot set you truly free
Until the chains that bind people
Are *smashed!*

Theirs are not metal chains
But mental chains
Of ignorance, greed, anger and stupidity.

Much harder are they to cut
For individual will is weak
Where lives of poverty abound,
And the courage to speak
Is sorely lacking in a tarnished world
Where money makes the world go round.

But I will fight and others too
To save your life from crowd and zoo;
To stop the drip of bile that bleeds you
To stop the dance that sorely grieves you
To ban the gun that seeks to skin you
To stop the dogs that tear within you,

So you can roam unfettered, free
With just respect and dignity
We'll educate humanity
And fight the world for *Libearty!*

Judith M Cangiano

BLACKEST CLOUDS

I try to understand every day why this world has to exist this way
his presumptuous smile just sitting on air it's transparent for you as
you've never been there, you can hardly stare in the face of despair if
it's a dress you've never had to wear

misunderstand you as I do remorseless life shines for you

Clearly isn't always just where it's at my friend you need to look a little
deeper than that, I used to think we all spoke the same language but
we're hanging in a state of languish

misunderstand you as I do remorseless life shines for you

In the blackest clouds you witness dying ones but I don't see many
people really trying, he's dragged across the coals by his face in chains
does his kind have to become extinct before we notice the pain?

misunderstand you as I do remorseless life shines for you

Too late to justify they've vanished to another place will there be an end
to this blood filled taste concede to the situation where the
definition's unknown.

Annette Marie Wilson

THE SAY OF THE JUNGLE BROTHERS

Praise to the World Society for the Protection of Animals.
To you are all the animals coming for protection.
When we are hunted, jailed, slaughtered, we run to you'
Come on - hurry in full force and fortify our territories!

We are satisfied with your reign and good deeds;
You are the only hope of the Animal Kingdom.
To the ends of the earth, of the furthest seas and oceans,
Already your protection is established.

Great is the World Society's wonderful plans and actions.
Through wisdom you are seriously educating the world.
You are carrying out God's responsibility given to man.
All animals on the earth and in the seas are in your care.

Oh Mother WSPA, our sovereign queen of the jungle,
For how long are your wicked brothers going to mistreat us?
Hopefully we have in addition, the Kindness Clubs going strong.
The jungle is full of joyful songs of praise to Mother WSPA.

Lawrence O Chongo

LIFE IN THE JUNGLE

A parrot sits in a tree,
Scanning the lush jungle below,
To see who he can see
As he glides away,
His colours kaleidoscope together,
With a different shade in every feather.

Noisily he flies through the
overgrown greenery,
Landing on a branch,
He sees a jaguar,
Its coat golden and jet, soft and sleek,
It lazily snoozes on the warm grass
as the sun sets.

In the late hours the jaguar is alert
and ready to pounce on its prey,
Making up for his laziness that day,
Whether he will get his treat of a
crocodile
        No one can say!

Emily Cressey (13)

A WISH FOR AN INDIAN ELEPHANT

I'd never seen a real elephant,
except at London zoo,
I'd often go and have a look
and see them grow and chew.

But then one day I felt so sad,
as I gazed at where they live.
A concrete enclosure, a muddy pool,
the moon's landscape was brighter than this.

I felt the tears well in my eyes
as I thought of where they're from
of a dense Indian forest,
that grew to the beat of a tabla drum.

If only I could make a spell.
I'd send them far away
I'd wish them to a lush green forest,
where they could run, and swim and play.

I'd introduce them to Ganesh,
the elephant-headed god,
They could twist their trunks in unison
Chew ghur, reflect and nod.

I wonder what they'd say to that?
'Let's go' I bet they'd say
This zoo is not my way of life
Only yours because you pay.

Johannah Fawthrop

PAWPRINTS

'Pawprints' my house is called,
   aptly named by one and all.
A guard dog we do not need,
   We have a terrapin indeed.
Sukie sits and watches out
   as Molly, our puppy, blunders about.
A Border collie is what she is,
   but oh she gets in such a tizz.
Tilly is our graceful cat,
   a tortoiseshell, so carefully sat.
Rupert and Katy go swimming by,
   I'm sure they're trying to say 'Hi.'
We have a rabbit, grey and white.
   Emily, with eyes so bright.
My animals mean the world to me.
No greater love could ever be.

Jane Lawton

UNTITLED

God will have no cruelty to living creatures or beings
No cruelty at all
For retribution there shall be, for inhumanity
When God's justice shall fall
The time it nears, it is not far away
For when God's angels shall hold sway
The justice ones and divinity angels
Each shall do their work
For God, they do not shirk
To end, what God will not have
The worthwhile ones to save.

R Postlethwaite

CRUELTY TO ANIMALS

They rubbed ointment on my back,
I was too weak, I could not attack,
And then they put liquid in my eyes,
I felt as if I should say my goodbyes.

But the ointment they kept adding,
And the liquid they kept dabbing,
Until at last I could not see,
Their infernal testing has brought an end to me.

They ended my life
For a few cosmetics.
But now I'm free from trouble and strife.
When they test on me, can't they see,
I have feelings too, and they can hurt me?

Jaymie Snowdon (11)

WHY?

I heard a tale that tore at my heart
It dug so deep, ripping me apart
Uncontrollable tears, rolling down my face
I will never understand, some of my fellow race!
With heavy heart, I look around and see
The destruction mankind has done to the trees
Rainforests torn down, not a bird in sight . . .
No thought for survival . . . now . . . the animals' plight!
Just for man's greed, what can compare
To the pain and torment of the majestic bear?
Cruelty abound, red hot pokers bored through
In searing pain, to dance - for you!
Trained on hot coals, remember their pain
Don't pay to see - don't let man gain.

Christine Peers

IMAGINE

I magine this, you are a bear. You're looked upon as a
traitor because of what you are. Your voice is never heard.
They are ready. Walking you out to a crowd of shouting hooligans.

M ade to face bull terriers with no teeth or claws.
Why have my teeth and claws been ripped out?
I did no-one any harm. They let the dogs out.
They are running to get me. I have no way to defend myself.

A ttacked, tortured, savaged. Why am I put through all this pain?
What will become of me at the end?
Will I be dead or maybe just half-dead.

G et out of here, must get out of here, but how? I'm trapped.
Why is a crowd of 10,000 hooligans cheering?
This is no game. This is my life, they're messing with.

I cannot explain the fear and confusion I have inside, for I have no voice

N o, I'm suffering in silence, like every animal has to.

E very hit gives agonising pain. 'Help! Help!' I cry.
Why doesn't anyone help me? Can my voice be heard?

Emily Sweet (14)

JUST

A beaver is just caught in a trap
Ten wolves are just left starving and bleeding
A hundred racoons just gnaw through their own limbs to be free
Ten million animals a year are just killed
Many species are just wiped out
A person just wears a fur coat.

Just?

Heather Sutch

MISHA (BRISTOL ZOO)

'Put distance between you', wise advise,
when confronted with one's only enemy - man.
Powerful jaws, strength of paws,
distance still, the only way one can,
hope to evade this beast called 'man'.
Thirty feet one way, twenty another,
is the maximum I can manage,
to avoid the damage,
man has in mind for me,
for I am confined you see, not free,
to wander the ice floes of thousands.
Where space, the elements, are my greatest weapons against man.
At his mercy I am trapped in this pit,
that is, in his eyes, a home from home.
White-washed, to hide the harshness of rock imitation,
water, a mere drop in the ocean,
is there, to complete the illusion,
or add to the confusion, of my mind,
in respect of mankind.
He has ensnared my body,
and, for the time being, my spirit,
but only until sleep,
whence my dreams deliver me unto freedom,
again to wander the ice floes of thousands.
The scent on the winds, devoid of taint,
I imagine too, that the walls of restraint,
are but the sheerness of natural ice,
formed by nature from material so cold,
beyond which will unfold
the way for me, to be.

In my hours of awakening, I realise
that mankind's deadliest weapon is his mind,
mental cruelty, just one of many things I find
he is capable of,
and yet, he speaks of love,
for all creatures great and small,
and here I am behind this wall.
But only until I sleep.
And when I sleep the sleep of sleeps,
and dream the dream of eternal dreams,
my spirit will be *free*
not chained or bound by humiliation or degradation,
or even idle curiosity.
When this release will happen, I cannot say,
a year tomorrow, perhaps one day.
The end, I can portend,
I will roam,
the ice floes of thousands.

Peter Gillard

ABERRATION

Do you go to see a circus
take your children and your wife,
and watch performing animals
live an un-natural life?

Don't you think they should have
dignity, freedom and their health,
instead of lining the pockets
of the ones who worship wealth?

When you go to see a circus
you support this cruelty.
So turn your back on the sawdust,
and set the animals free.

Daf Richards

Now... And Then

You are clever, you have power
You can make or you can break.
You have marvellous potential
You can choose the path you take.

        I have no such choice before me
        I must live just for the hour
        I must walk the path of nature
        I have feelings but no power.

You could banish the world starvation
You could heal the sick and lame
But money's more desirable
And murder's done for gain.

        I have no worldwide ambitions
        I am happy just to live
        I have naught for trade or barter
        Only love, and that I give.

Yet I would live beside you
I would trust you if I could,
Though you abuse my friendship
And you often spill my blood.

        But, He who sees each sparrow fall
        And knows each stab of fear
        And feels the silent agonies,
        Which no-one else can hear.

Will interweave our destinies
Into His Perfect Plan
Though I am just an animal
And you, of course, are Man.

And when our souls come face to face
On that advancing day
Which one will stand and shine and which
For shame, will turn away?

Tricia Sturgeon

THE DOG - MAN'S BEST FRIEND!

What a friend we all have - a dear friend!
A dog, so sincere and friendly,
A faithful friend alert and lovely.
Ready to guard anything under the cloud.
Sniffing around - always in a good mood.

Listen, all people of the world,
Members and non-members of the Kindness Clubs,
Give the dog your love and not a slap,
Kindness from your hearts, not a harsh word.
He will always appreciate this.

Feed him a balanced diet,
Never feed yourselves on dogs' fat and meat,
Never on left-overs and dirty, smelly foods.
Many will be pleased in their hearts,
And many will be left in thought.

Many are left lonely and unattended,
Roaming the villages, licking dirty bones,
Fighting over rotten meat and dry horns.
Thin, sick and wild, longing for any food,
Yet tough, keen and very bold.

He is a friendly and honest guard,
Yet fed on nothing but poisoned food.
Better than the watchman at the gate,
Who turns against you out of hate.
Many have died of hunger, sickness and hate.

Mary Asonga

THE MYTH OF THE GREEN BEAR

In the green myths of the green wood
That are told
Of the great green bear
No mention of death or danger
Or running for your life
Was there.

In those green days, the Orinocco bear
Was loved and blessed
Lime, emerald or jade
They knew the sun would always shine
While the green bear made jest.

Smiles from the green bears yellow eyes
Were said to make you mellow
Wise and drive out cold
And bees gave up their honey
In sunlit ritual
Exchanging gold for gold.

In those green days
Of that lost Orinocco wood
Jokes were currency
There was no bad or good
Long hours were taken up
With tickling and listing
All the words for laughter
Carved with a gentle claw
On branches low enough
For bear cubs
Rolling on the forest floor.

For the coming of the pancake moon
To celebrate the spring
They'd steal strange carapaces
The butterflies cocoon
And sit round in a ring to watch
And wait the foggy hours till dawn
They'd rock and croon
Until the sun rose hot
And baking on the forest lawn.

Then crick, crack, rustle and a pop
All heads would start
All eyes would follow
The little wet bright sheets
That darted like the swallow
'Up, up until no more they'd sigh
And count the coloured pieces
Of the moon her mother sun
Draws up to dry.

On wet and wintry days the tribe
Would meet in caves
Beneath the forest floor to sing
The sun back from her feather nest
On instruments of cuttlefish
And string they played the best
Gifts from the forest saw
To their every need
Paid for by choruses and harmony.

Not till came whispers
Probably the birds with some sly song
Did doe eyes slit
And love dissolve to greed
Green faded in the trees that season
Slumber fell too fast
And stayed too long
Waking all was altered, all was gone.

Now spun the choking tent moth
Swarmed the scale
Now moss was mould and footsteps
Left a slimy trail
Trees clung together yellow leafed
Practising adieux
Dead bees crunched underfoot
Lifeless with lost allure.

In empty forests now
Where dead trees knock and slumber
On odd days when the wind is still
These, some ghostly shadows lumber
A song, a breath of laughter parts the shade
And insects hiss and spit and argue
Dark as thunder
Over which was best
Lime, emerald or jade.

Berta R Freistadt

GUN LICENCE

There they go again - the guns.
Their staccato voices nag the stillness.
Like a well trained chorus line the hunters
Raise their weapons to the violent sky.
Their insignificance is minimised.
Manhood proved.
This is better than sex.

Ripped savagely from the air
The desperate birds can beg for no reprieve.
Nor expect it.

Paddy Phillips

A Letter To Man: The Jungle Cry

If only you could feel it,
You noble men who walk,
How it feels to be hurt so many times,
I am sure you would not like it.
How painful it is as a bullet tears through your tissues,
Wriggling in pain as you die;
Just for your skin, teeth, tusks and even our claws!
Don't you see we've enabled you to see the outside people?
To get a lot of money when your fellows come to see us?
Yet the only reward you can offer is brutal death.
It's not fair, it's just not a fair game to treat a 'friend' so bad.
How we wish you could appreciate us, please let us live to marvel at
What goes on around you and us.
I am just an animal, no different from the others,
That is why I plead just for peace between you and us
By putting behind us all the shooting.

Well, it's true we can't conserve ourselves.
That is why we ask for your protection and we promise to do you good.
As I speak for the jungle, I know my fellow animals are already happy,
As they hope we'll have a contract of conservation soon.
They all ask you to listen to them,
To listen to their jungle cry that has been passed from former
                                        generations
For they hope this time that beggars will ride horses
As their wishes become so clearly true.

Think about us,
Please conserve us,
As we are tired of the war.
Remember - I am speaking for the jungle.

Your friend,
Chief of Animals.

Christine Khasina

A Tale For Three Bears

'Write me a poem concerning bears.'
Said she whose word is law.
(Do children know what grace is theirs
As they pause at Granddad's door?)

'Whence the need for Ursine Verse?'
My tone was fittingly gruff.
'There's Paddington, Rupert and Winnie the Pooh,
Come, surely that is enough!'

She closed the door and clasped my hand,
Then, eyeing me most severely,
Declared, 'You know those bears aren't real . . .
Well, Pooh is, sometimes, nearly!'

'A noble animal, much be-smirched,
In ditty or narrative rhyme.
A poem for Bruin must be researched,
We'll try to be thorough, this time.'

To follow my thesis we duly rose,
And flew like the early lark,
To board the conveyance which hourly goes,
To a stop near Regents Park.

'This way to the monkeys, the parrots is there,
The lion-'ouse, camels and ferrets,
But if the young miss wants to gaze at a bear,
You must climb up the Mappin Territs.'

We followed the Keeper of Concrete Mounds,
In his neat brown suit and bowler,
And high on the terrace accordingly found,
The kodiak, brown and polar.

The kodiak posed for a camera shot,
While the brown bear went to kip.
Blue was the pool and the sun was hot,
As the polar submerged for a cooling dip.

'Roosevelt's teddy was not quite right,
The nose is a little too snub,
But the Himalay bear is a lovely sight,
With its shy and tiny cub.'

Myth and reality duly blend,
When you get the poetry right . . .
'But the polar and granddad are my best friend,
For they both have hair that is yellowish-white!'

John Guy

THE ANIMALS AND MAMMALS

How do you feel about the animals?
Do you really care
To see them in small cages,
So that you can stare?
Would like to see them free,
Like the mammals of the sea,
They swim free, a lovely sight to see,
As they seem to glide around,
Happy as can be.
Sometimes, wish it was me,
Cannot swim you see,
Think about the animals that are
               in cages in the zoo,
Lions, tigers, gorillas,
Looking out at you,
Wishing I am sure, they were you,
Being in an enclosure where people
               could see them roam,
Be with their own kind happy to play around,
That's what I would like to see,
In their own ground roam free.

E Browning

OCTOBER DOOM

I hear the dogs, I hear the horn, I know the time is near.
Somewhere a fox lies all forlorn, transfixed and full of fear.

She knows the sound, her belly aches, she quivers with the pain,
She must keep on alert for all their sakes, these dogs are not too tame!

The raucous horn is pitched so high, it's tinny and it's loud,
None of the pack will miss its call as round the men they crowd.

Today the rabbits and the stoat, pigeons and pheasants fine
Have no need to fear their coats, it's not their lives on the line.

Macabre followers on foot, their cars lining the grass verges,
Binoculars ready to enjoy the sight, filling some primal urges.

As the vixen and her family take flight, horses, spittle flecked nostrils
                                                          quivering
The dogs are mud spattered and bold, our fox hides her brush all a
                                                          shivering.

They want her brush, she need not be told,
She runs through fields and hedges
She's very tired, breathless and sore,
Quietly though terrified, through battered corn, she edges.

Red jackets blazing in October's grey light
Women pristine in their hunting gear.
They shout and goad dogs with all of their might.
Whips crack, hooves thud, our fox feels such fear.

The older ones have experience of this,
It happens at this time of season.
But the young are so green, they preamble in bliss,
They are caught, killed without any reason.

I don't know how anyone can take these lives,
Hounding with such sweet pleasure.
Enjoying the chase and the fear; torturing
And killing something we treasure.

Today's hunt is over, fields all churned up,
Horses winded, dogs breathless,
They've finished drinking the hunting cup
Given up for now, this fox was not reckless.

Dorothea Carroll

A BUDDHIST PRAYER

My Lord Avalokiteshvara, with one thousand arms,
Please let's all feel your compassion, your balm.

There's

The snow leopard who live their life in Tibet,
And the tiny feline, the cat, who's a pet.
The wolf, fox, the companion dog,
Pot-bellied pig and wild wart-hog.
Mouse, rat, ferret, coypu, mink,
Striped tiger, cheetah, lion and lynx.
The elephant, buffalo, bison and deer,
Eagle, penguin and white polar bear.
Brown bear, gorilla, lemur, monkey,
Skunk, hare, rabbit, badger, donkey.
The lamb, ox, cattle, man and horse,
Zebra, hippopotamus and rhinoceros, of course.
Woodpecker, kingfisher, otter and vole,
Beaver, hedgehog, squirrel and mole.
All birds who give to the Earth their song,
Swan, moorhen and mallard who swim along.
The whale, the dolphin and fish of the sea,
Butterfly, dragonfly and honeybee.
Koala, platypus and kangaroo,
All who live free or caged in a zoo.

Lord of Compassion, named here are only a few -
Please hold all sentient beings safe, in the knowledge of you.

Anita Richards

The Fifth Commandment

When our heavy wings first flapped upward,
Dull eyes, raised from the swamp, saw suddenly a larger world.
Later, cautious ears, turning from the carcass,
Heard something never heard before, -
Not danger, or the dawn wind, -
It murmured, spread and sparkled in the canopy,
As our children flexed their feathered throats.
A first breath; the sky lightened.

We invented happiness; it isn't difficult.
Live quietly with your family, shun the neighbours;
Roll with the seasons; watch the youngsters grow
From milky spring to feasting summer;
Fish, easy in the river; honey, sweet in the forest;
Forever time to splash and swim, to tumble in the early snow.
Sniff the hard ice in the wind; time for bed.
You will have slept, clutching our pompous image, in your infant
                                                                       happiness.

My first thoughts were yours.
I thought: this stick will reach the hidden food;
These leaves will make a shelter from the rain;
A group is stronger that a family,
Running, swinging, searching together.
I consoled my brother, we shared the fruit;
I stretched upright to reach a branch,
And saw further.

You have forgotten who we are, and what we did;
With knowledge came the loss of wisdom.
Trees fall, the empty river dwindles, and the snow melts;
The nests are scattered, and the caves empty;
All sweetness gone, the jar is broken.
The wind's returning breath brings only dust,
And agony echoing from steel walls.
A sudden sinking feeling . . .
                            Where is my brother?
Our mothers and fathers were yours;
Honour your ancestors.

Diana Oxford

BEAR CUB

Once I had a happy home,
Free to run and free to roam,
As a cub I had no other,
But the love of my mother.

And then they came large and tall,
Slaughtering the one to whom I was born,
Then I was roped and dragged away,
The pain is still with me even today.

The red hot coals they made me dance,
I didn't really stand a chance
Men who thought it very funny,
To keep a dancing bear for money.

When will society start to see,
This is not the life for me?
Once I had a happy home,
Free to run and free to roam.

There's little more to be said.
My only wish is that I was dead.

P Lopez

THE CRY OF THE ANIMALS

My ideal world would be one that would be,
Full of animals, all roaming free.
Where forests are alive with the sound of birds,
And elephants are seen, herd upon herd.

But instead, despite all the bans,
The humans arrive with their evil plans.
Animals do no harm as they amble along,
But suddenly they can sense something wrong.
The danger they sense will ultimately pave
The way to a dismal, doom laden grave.

The yelp of hounds fill the foxes' ears;
Nothing can seem to quell its fears.
Heart pounding, slowly running out of breath,
Knowing it's coming ever closer to death.

Poachers stalk and try to slaughter for,
The creature's exquisite fur and their paw.
The noble head, the majestic face,
Expelled forever, thanks to the human race.

Faster and faster the whales are dying,
Nothing seems to stop that harpoon from flying.
A day's hunting over, the whales catch their breath
While the other half have all been massacred to death!

Cramped into crates, from the wild they're caught,
Only to be traded, shipped, sold or bought.
All dignity lost, their lives full of sorrow,
Who knows if they will still be alive tomorrow?

The trauma animals suffer fills them with panic,
As they run blindly from all things mechanic.
The pain they feel is a pain like no other,
Once their lives are over they won't have another.

All they want is to have a contented life;
They can't while hunted by man and his knife,
Who listens gleefully to the crack of the gun,
And watches the animals lying there, defeated and numb.

What is happening, we all must dread
The day all animals wind up dead.
Extinction is forever, so why can't we see,
The ones who can stop it are you and me?

Every single day of the week,
The animals' future becomes more bleak.
In a circle of life there will become a space,
No longer will we witness their awe inspiring grace.
We can't let this happen; it was not meant to be,
All animals should be liberated and free!

Rosemarie Scott

A Happier Me

There's not much in this life for free
But there's one thing that makes for a happier me
I gather stale bread, scraps and the like
And to my local park, I head for a hike
They are always there, never tired of waiting
For the goodies I bring, they've been anticipating.
Ducks, swans, there's birds of all kinds
I feed them whilst trying to read their minds
I love to watch them, as they taste my wares
In this world of troubles, have they any cares?
Our lives are so different, theirs seem so serene
But then I'm not a bird, and that pond's not so clean
And so my goodies, they must come to an end
But I leave after making, every bird a friend
There's not much in this life for free
But I know how to make for a happier me!

Lynn Greene

THE SWAN

This winged perfection of the air,
whose whiteness would put snow to shame,
emitting only the quietest sound
admired by so many on the ground.

Ponds, lakes, all are graced by you.
Anger is not your trait.
Proud and beautiful, you sail serenely by
ignoring others with your head held high.

When you and yours take to flight
men stop, and gaze at this wondrous sight.
Not a word is uttered as you rise up high
till you become a speck against the sky.

If man would emulate your family care,
oh what joys he'd find there.
Not for you a broken tryst,
for you a life together is a must.

Do not I pray you pass the vision by,
but see as with a painter's eye,
this creature of Elysian perfection.

Tony Vanner

EDWARD

I'm Edward, I'm a grand old fellow,
The years have passed and made me mellow,
I've lived nearly a century
And I've seen lots of history.

Young bears may have more energy
But I've experience you see -
I've shared so many hopes and fears,
I've joined in fun and soaked up tears.

My coat's a little sparse because
I've always had my share of hugs,
But please don't think I'm going bald -
Just more distinguished as I get old.

These days, as I sit or lie
And watch the world as it goes by
I think its fun that in old age
I have become again 'the rage'!

Jayne-Louise Herbert

A PUPPY CALLED BENGY

So small, forever by my side,
Sending out love to each soul spied.
Loud raucous youth and timid child,
Those who walked by and those who smiled,
            To everyone.

He greets them all with bounding joy,
And rushes to old man or boy.
He does not think he may be spurned,
Expects always some love returned
            From everyone.

So small, a friend to all is he,
Who sleeps in trust upon my knee.
No thought of fear disturbs his rest,
This little dog who sees the best
            In everyone.

Oh when he's old and cannot leap,
In joyous greeting, may he keep
This love and trust he gaily gives.
May he always, while he lives
            Love everyone.

Nancy Bryant

Please

Please give a thought to all our animals
And for them shed a tear
Because of human cruelty
Our animals live in fear
They live in cruel cages
Are trapped in walls of death
From which they can't escape at all
And cannot catch their breath
Living goats do christen boats
With their warm blood in Indonesia
Parrots in tubes cannot spread their wings
Cannot escape their seizure
All over the world our animals die
No mercy is shown by man
So please shed a tear for our animals
And help them as fast as you can
All over the world they're mistreated
It's so sad that man is so cruel
So sad for the animals suffering
So sad they are used as a tool
The animals captured and helpless
Know torture and pain for life
These creatures are hapless and don't stand a chance
All they know is pain and strife
So please shed a tear for our animals
Show sweet mercy so they may live
A life without pain and torture
It is time for us all to give
Is it really too much to ask for?
In all conscience how can you say no
To a plea for help for these creatures?
Please give them a chance to a life without woe
Imagine a world without them
How terrible it would be
If in all this world there was only
The likes of you and me

Imagine no whales, no tigers nor dolphins
No monkeys, no bears to be seen
What a world this would be with just you and me
And pictures of what once had been
So hasten to help all our creatures
For without them our world would be
A place oh so barren and empty
With nothing at all left to see.

Clare Marshall

MY BEST FRIEND
(Dedicated to my beloved dog 'Jessie')

I found you shivering at my door, a cowering body, a frightened face
You were cold and hungry, your coat was a disgrace.
I bathed you and I nursed you, I fed you well each day.
And as the days passed by, I knew that you would stay.

I had to teach you right from wrong, you didn't have a clue.
But you were always keen to please, I in turn rewarded you.
No more digging up the garden, or chewing shoes - I'd get upset!
Through constant love and patience, I found my ideal pet.

We have walked in summer sunsets, we have played in winter snow
I explored wooded valleys, always with you in tow.
We waded into mountain streams, we frolicked in the sea.
You are always by my side, I'm glad that you found me.

In those years which passed us by, we shared both good and bad.
You lay your head upon my lap, whenever I am sad.
In times of joy you dance around with wagging little tail.
You seem to know my every mood, your devotion does not fail.

Now, a check up at the vets today, reveals your heart is weak.
No more long walks, no chocolate drops, the future's looking be bleak.
So by the firelight, here we sit, together to the end.
For I would not desert you now, my faithful little friend.

Margaret A French

COME TO ME MOTHER SEAL

Come to me Mother Seal,
Shed you tears, your child is dead,
Clubbed to death yet again
For the vanity and greed of Man.

They who do this thing are blind
They see not the soul that lies behind
The coat so sleek and given free
To give you warmth from snow and sea.

They cannot see the love you hold
For children born in bitter cold
Nor do they see as they do thrust,
Eyes so young and full of trust.

They cannot see your futile plea
To leave your child beneath your breast
Nor do they see your gentleness
And total lack of self-defence.

They do not stay to see your grief
Or view the carnage they have wrought,
Babies torn for bloody pay
That you must live with now each day.

Come to me Mother Seal,
I will share your grief with you,
We will pray for spirits now
Safe with God and whole again.

When I leave, this pledge I give,
To share this deed with all who'll hear,
Your children's coats I will not buy
So shed my conscience of your cry.

One fisherman I'll seek to find
Whose eyes and soul I will un-blind,
Who'll seek in turn amongst his brothers
To end this kill and pain to Mothers.

Linda Roth

DOWN BY THE WATER-HOLE

Down by the water-hole in dusty Africa
A herd of elephants are bathing,
Not a rustle, not a sound; silence fills the air
But the scorched landscape is stirring.

A matriarch coaxes a tiny calf
Fills up her trunk and flicks away flies
While watching nearby, a majestic bull
Basks under deep blue African skies.

Caught on the wind, Man's scent rises
Hunters with rifles make their presence known
The troubled herd shield their squealing babies
Out of the silence, shots ring and elephants moan.

First one, then two are brought crashing to the ground
Yet the murderer's work is not yet done,
With thrusting knives they steal the great white tusks
Blood-stained ivory glistens in the sun.

Down by the water-hole in dusty Africa
The smell of death is all that remains,
Magnificent creatures are slaughtered in their prime
Man's greed wreaks havoc on Africa's plains.

So please in the name of humanity,
Lets completely ban the sale of ivory!

Katherine Delaney

LADY BLUE

Queen of the woods and the moors.
A fearless warrior has returned from an ephemeral grave.

The nightfall has come and has arisen
the silent ghost, so she may tread the
leafy paths of the moonlit glade once more.

Silver shines the coat of the majestic vixen.
Lady Blue in a wood of winter shades.

The message sweeps the muted glen,
Undergrowth of a thousand eyes breathes
cautiously, as the sapphire shadow graces
its path for a single second, and halts,
ears pricked, nose pointed to the heavens.

The soft whiteness of the night, silhouettes
the magnificent animals slender figure,
as she waits patiently for movement
within the shadowy forest.

The deathly silence is broken
only by a single beast.

Unaware of the lingering fate ahead of
him, the tiny rodent tenses,
and springs into the sharp rimmed black
hole, which is to finalise his doom.

Hunger is no more, and the victorious beast turns,
and dissolves into the remaining gloom.

The rose sky of day, on the horizon,
signals life can return to the wood once more.

The trees can stretch again.

Tannsey Palmer

THE STRAYS

The trust is there
It's in their eyes
It's in the air
Of wanting to belong to someone.
Someone who would really care.

The hope is clear
The wait goes on
The step comes near
But moves along and slowly fades.
Fades until no-one can hear.

They took us home
When we were young
But love just died
And we were cast aside and left to roam.
Roam and now we are alone.

Sonia Griffiths

BEARS

Bears are wonderful things,
Roaming black, white and brown
Wonders of the world, which
Makes the seven wonders of the world eight.
Fur matted, face pierced, faces covered in
Blood, is what bears which are bated go through.
Dancing bears are no better off
Having to walk on red hot metal,
Burning feet, rope rubbing the inside
Of the jaw, chains nailed in to
The sides of the body,
Torture, anger, *pain*.

Max Wakefield

MORNING SUN

The dawn breaking
Is the love of the earth unfurled
The sun rising in the east
From under the edge of the world

On the very first day of summer
Cool, pale, washed dawn
And somewhere
Intermittent birds sing
From drifting hawthorn
Before the world's heart beats
Cold in a hollow
Empty blue skies
With the promise of heat

A transient fox
Mirage of life
Twitches the brush
And broom in the copse

Queen of the woodland
Coo-coos in the silence
Bobtails and wagtails
Hopping the distance
Between buttercups waving
Their yellow bloom
And daisies as big as
The reflected moon
Now sleeping

Quiet flutter. Rise
Cool breeze
Early butterflies
Seek out the best places
And move
From stem to stem
Like wishes
In the hearts of men

This midsummer's day
Is just begun
We rise together
Daughter and sun

Rachel A Kruft

MERCY RESCUE

My chain is so heavy, the air very hot
Surely the humans haven't let me to rot?
The silence is eerie, no voice can be heard
And the heat is making my eyes very blurred.

I feel pangs of hunger, my throat is so dry
I whimper with terror, but I know not why.
'Listen' a strange rumble I don't understand
Why I am left in this desolate land.

Where are the children who would give me a bone?
Please someone help me, I feel so alone.
Out of the shadows, I hear sounds of feet
I listen with joy, my heart skips a beat.

'Hello old pal,' a drink is a must,
Then gentle hands stroke me, I feel I can trust
This comforting voice, of him I've no fears
I lick his face, and I am licking his tears.

My life is now serene and calm
I walk with my master free from harm.
So please fellow creatures, do not despair
I know for you also there are humans who care.

Patricia E M Ayres

The Zebra Finch

The malnutritional figure of the sick creature
Lies in the corner of the cell.
His arms left limp from the injury he bares,
His legs are rendered useless as he can't find the energy to function.
He rocks his head slowly from side to side,
This his only comfort.
His shoulder bulges over normality and stretches
His thin skin beyond comfort.
He lives on, unaware that his arm could at any moment
Explode and his insides begin to slowly pour down his chest.

He whimpers and squirms across the cold, concrete floor
Lined with his own excrement,
In a pathetic, unrewarding attempt to find food.
His innocent eyes ask so many questions,
But his deteriorated brain wouldn't understand
The answers.
Through his bars, he looks on to the world
In anticipation and false hope.
If his brain would allow, he would wonder.
If his limbs would move, he would try to escape.
If his heart would say how it felt, he would be sad.

Yet this creature has been a prisoner
Of his own breed forever. A murderer in his own right,
He does not possess such qualities and does not wish to.
His brain is dead,
His limbs are paralysed,
His heart dumb.
His memory tells him of the time he was born,
His cell was larger, warmer then,
He had food and friends.
Even Memory is fading.

Now he is just an empty soul,
Paralysed and forgotten.
His only ambition is death.
The only sign that life remains is the
Ticking of his heart and the gleam in his eye.
He can't wait for the day when, finally
He is relieved of these burdens
That keep him in the land of the living
And his life of torture comes to an end.

Helen Wildbore

A BROWN BEAR IN ALBANIA

Back and forth he paces, back and forth;
Neither turning his head nor watching
Who peers through the bars.

In a dingy cage in a dingy building;
Doomed to pace back and forth
With only a few hairs on his naked body.

I'll never forget the brown bear,
Captive in a dirty concrete cage,
In a pathetic zoo in Albania.

It was too late to save him;
He died during the conflicts -
From cold, from lack of care - from ignorance?

'It's a relief' we said, 'He's out of pain.'
But how many other beasts still
Pace back and forth, back and forth in captivity?

Elizabeth Wallace

LEST WE FORGET

Lest we forget this November day
For all who died in wars, we pray.

Lest we forget, let us pray some more
For those other victims of man made war.
Those innocent 'others' who have no voice
Who share our earth but free from choice.

Lest we forget man's best friend
Courageous and loyal right up to the end.
Man went to war with misguided pride
This loyal companion by his side
Willing to follow where e'er he must
With adoring eyes and total trust
Ready to sacrifice his all
Lay down his life to his master's call.

Lest we forget our hardworking friends
Who in times of war man depends
Pulling our wagons against all odds
Beneath their feet no fresh green sods
Just mud and blood where fields once lay
With cannons roar to greet the day,
Donkeys and mules from origins humble
Toiling all day with never a grumble
Whipped or cursed and often abused
Let us pray for equine misused.

Lest we forget our pets who bore
Our grief and hardship through the war
They licked our tears and helped us through
The darkest days and night-times too
They brought us joy in our despair
Comforting us . . . by being there.
Lest we forget.

Joan Ann Knipe

THOUGHTS

W hen will all bears be free,
   free from all the tyranny.
   We should all take a stance,
   against people who would make them dance.

S top the hurt and the cruelty,
   let them live, let them be.
   In peace and tranquillity,
   a joy for us all to see.

P rotect them in their wild ways,
   with freedom all of their days.
   To sleep in peaceful dreams,
   of salmon leaping, splashing streams.

A s we live from day to day,
   we forget the price these creatures pay.
   Paws! for thoughts, think and prey,
   that all bears will be free one day.

Lynn Gibbons

THEY REMEMBER

Taken away at an early age.
To be exploited or used for trade.
Badly treated, tortured, they suffer.
Man has no respect for the life of another.

They live lives of agony, excruciating pain.
In captivity, never to roam free again.
The appalling conditions in which they sleep
The memories within their hearts
Forever remain so deep, so deep.

Amanda Dinnivan (14)

THE PHILOSOPHER

The moment was all so magic that
I can't remember
If I touched you,
I think I must.
Both of us, so alone but
Never could be lonely
Though far away
At sea.
Some moments last forever, they
Are of pain.
Why do hours of joy
Seem like seconds?
I never knew whether you were
Father or Mother,
You were silent
On the theme.
Yet communication was apparent
No words were needed
To share the spell
Of being.
You gave me more that I could
Possibly have given . . .
Dreamed of in
Your philosophy.
I had to wrench myself away
And leave you there
To meditate
The meaning of life . . .
King Penguin.

Angela M Baber

Cargoes Of Innocence

I've left my farm where I've been since a lamb,
I've left the grass where I could eat all I can,
I'm with my friends, we're all huddled together,
In a room with bars, that doesn't keep out the weather.

I look at my friends, their eyes are full of panic,
I look outside and wonder at the racket.
I see people shouting and holding banners high,
Why are we here? Why? Why, Why?

I feel this violence is something to do with us,
The people fighting and making a fuss,
The men with helmets and bright yellow jackets,
Straining to hold the people back, trying to stop the racket.

I feel they are trying to help us poor sheep,
But somehow I fear we will our appointment keep.
Thank you people for your trouble, thank you for your concern,
You've started a battle from which many will learn.

We are on the sea now, still in our crates,
If only we know the end of our fate,
But perhaps it is better that we do not know
Where we are heading and where we will go.

I do not understand why you were there,
But please still offer up a little prayer,
We're not little lambs who have gone astray,
We are grown up sheep who do not know the way.

Some have to suffer and many to die,
My mother told me this, I don't know why,
For man must fill his stomach and a profit make,
But there are good and bad, she said, make no mistake.

And so again I thank you although *our* fate is sealed,
Carry on the good work until all is revealed.

Marian Allen

TRAPPED

Lonely hours behind these bars
waiting for the dawn
soulless hours . . . endless days
spent pacing to and fro
oh just to be that butterfly
a-nestling on the grass
to run again thro' woods and streams
loving the leaves and dust
to feel the wind and rain once more
the heat of the summer's sun
oh what a joy, sleep under stars
the frolic . . . hunt . . . and fun
the waking when the dawning comes
with frost upon the air
but I am here, a man's delight
captured . . . caged . . . defeated
my only joy a small child's bun
given when Mr Bear is seated.

Harold Brawn

DOG'S LIFE

A dog; four legs, a tail, a tongue and some ears,
Any colour; black, brown, red, blonde, multiple,
The size; little and cute or big and ugly,
Oh! what decisions.
The life; cold and hard or warm and soft,
A bed, a bowl, food and pats.
No work, the boredom, the garden, the walks,
The pub, the orders, *Sit, Stop, Stay.*
Oh! the confusion.
Oh what it is to be a dog!
Not so good all of the time, eh!

Diane Spreadborough

ABANDONED

The little children playing
They do not see me here
I have no strength to whimper
Or wipe away a tear
I was a happy little puppy
But my owners grew fed up
As my tiny paws grew large
I was no longer 'their little pup'
Just like some rubbish
I was thrown out on the street
I need someone to care for me
I need some food to eat
I have not given up quite yet
So please, please see me here
And give me strength to whimper
And forget about my tears.

Lisa Bennett

SHALL WE DANCE

Rings on her fingers, bells on her toes
This bear will have music, wherever she goes
But this bear is not asking to dance in the street
Nor is she happy with sore, aching feet.

This bear detests cages, so cramped and confined
And with chains through her body, no comfort she'll find
She does not want laughter each time she falls down
They may break her spirit, but she is nobody's clown

This bear wants her freedom, to roam and to play
To bask in the sunshine, eat fresh plants every day
A walk through the forest, feel the wind on her face
This bear really needs *you*, to get on her case.

Marguerite Piper

FOR BILLIE

Oh small brown dog.
The fear I saw in your huge eyes,
As you peered out at me,
From within your cold dirty prison cell.
Two paws placed on a ledge,
Your nose pressed through the bars of your confinement.
Oh small brown dog, did I choose you?
Or did you choose me?

Now, medium sized dog.
Your paws are growing larger,
That I can see.
My slippers lying in tatters.
All daily routines are beginning to change for me.
What did I release from that prison?
Oh medium sized dog, did I choose you?
Or did you choose me?

Oh! Very large and boisterous brown dog.
Who chases my poor cats from room to room.
Upturns and chews things, when left on her own.
Eats everything and anything
That isn't nailed to the ceiling.
Your paws are growing *larger*! brown dog.

But wait!
You run, play and give me endless hours of fun.
You'd never hurt me,
Make promises that you couldn't possibly hope to keep.
Invade my private space when I want to be alone.
Or irritate and bore me.

Oh. Brown dog.
Whether you chose me,
Or I chose you,
I welcome you into my life, Billie.

Irene Reddish

ALL GOD'S CREATURES

I've written to my MP
and asked him to support
the bill to banish hunting
that most cruel and evil sport.

How can man condone
the taking of a life
in such a cruel fashion
and causing so much strife.

One cannot blame the hounds
for their part in the deed;
they are but God's dumb creatures,
trained to satisfy man's need.

The hunt set out at dawning
resplendent on their steeds,
with no thought for the poor fox
as in throes of death he bleeds.

Then let us be united
in our fight to do what's right,
and forever ban this cruel sport
as we recognise the fox's plight.

Ruth Barclay Brook

CAN'T BEAR TO LOOK

Don't walk away, without a glance,
For he can't sing and he won't dance.
Stop for a while . . . and memorise
The fear and pain within his eyes.
Reach out and save his dignity,
Give him hope, and set him free.

Elaine Simmons

GREY WOLF

Night falls,
On a land carpeted in snow.
The crescent moon comes unbidden, shining down to leave the snow
sparkling like diamonds cast on white velvet.
Through the darkness she appears, in one fluid movement, belly low,
skimming the crunching ground.
She glides through the cobweb shadows cast down by leafless trees,
a ghostly presence, silver, grey and white.
She stands erect in the bleak, raw landscape, captured in moonlight.
Observing the night with peridot eyes, velvety snout lifted in the
foggy air, alert and searching.
Her thick winter fur quivers, dusted with powdery snow.
A long, noble face raises up to the skies, mouth opening,
The song is released to puncture the silence, haunting melody
which echoes unhindered through spidery branches and caverns
of stone. Resounding.
All around her, mounds of snow erupt in powdery explosions as
the pack awake, respond to the call of the hunt.
Shake frost from their fur and join in the chorus until silence
is banished and replaced with the howls.
The leader lopes off, like a silver bullet, the musky smell of
deer in her nostrils.
The pack end their song and follow the chase, darting through
the trees, through shadow and moonlight, dark, graceful bodies
slung low, eyes burning with golden firelight.
Night time fills with the thunder of a hundred paws on hard-packed
snow, the excited, impatient snapping of muzzles, the crazed
yipping of the young and uncertain.
Their breath comes in hot, steamy clouds to be swallowed by
the frigid air.
Grey wolf.
Once misunderstood, derided and hunted,
Now the symbol for all that is wild, and all
That is free.

J M Park

THE CRY

His mother killed before his eyes,
a brilliant light in the young cub dies.
Forced into a life filled with misery and pain,
dragged through filthy streets, beatings with a cane.
>For the lovely paying people, *'Dance! Dance! Dance!'*
>Pulled, prodded, punched, *'Prance! Prance! Prance!'*

Hour upon hour in the scorching heat,
walking, dancing - beaten into defeat.
The hours, the days, the months and each year,
and soon the cub becomes a full-grown bear.
>For the lovely paying people, *'Dance! Dance! Dance!'*
>Pulled, prodded, punched, *'Prance! Prance! Prance'!*

Given little water, rotting food to eat,
dragged through the streets in the steaming heat.
A dancing bear delights the crowd,
they laugh and clap and shout out loud.
>For the lovely paying people *'Dance! Dance! Dance!'*
>Pulled, prodded, punched, *'Prance! Prance! Prance!'*

Amidst the crowd's laughter, in a painful wail,
the bear cries out in a cry so frail.
'Someone, please save me from this life of hell,
take me back to the life I once knew so well.
Where the grass grows thick and the air is sweet,
where there are no hot pavements to scorch my feet.
Please take me back to the life I knew well,
Someone . . . please save me from this life of hell!'

A stranger heard the cry as he passed that way;
thank the Lord that stranger was from WSPA . . .

Lilian Gillard

BORN TO BE FREE

When you see me dancing
Do not laugh and cheer
Look a little deeper
You will see my fear.

When you come to stroke me
Touch me once again
Look hard into my deep, dark eyes
And you will see my pain.

I am a fearsome animal
Bought down onto my knees
Money is the reason why
I am taught to dance - to please.

I was not born a dancing bear
I was born to hunt and roam
Not in this God forsaken place
But in wilderness called home.

I was not born to live my life
In harsh captivity
I was born to walk the land
Born to be free.

Verity Holsgrove

SANCTUARY

Gently I lead you
Away from hurt and pain
Gently I'll heal you
Make you whole again

Clouded eyes of torment
Dulled by silent tear
Your soul has been broken
By cruelty, torture, fear

Softly I hold you
Feel you tremble from your pain
Softly I whisper
I'll make you well again

Little one as I watch you
Peaceful in your sleep
I'll love and protect you
Your trust I'll always keep

Chrissie

ANIMALS OF THE WORLD

Why must animals suffer
Purely for human gain,
They live, they breathe, just like us
And they feel the pain.

Baby animals are torn away
From their mother's grasp,
Please stop and have a think to yourself
This is all that we ask.

If animals could rule the world
And have their very own say,
They would really make us suffer
They would make us pay.

So let's make a stand to help them out
The whole world must unite,
For animals really need our help
Let's not go down without a fight.

They need animal charities to give support
And animal lovers like us,
Or animals will disappear
We won't see them for dust.

Marilyn Dunne

BEAUTY THE HORSE

Snow fell in October last year,
The wagon was summoned, it is my
gravest fear.
Appears like a monster, foot of the hill,
slithering, screeching, here for the kill.
The snow was my solace, sent by the Lord,
Ice insurmountable, cattle truck roared.

My future lies in the abattoir or sales
Selling myself, or all has failed!
My fate becomes a bolt in the brain
Hauled by a chain to a rack -
Butchered, then used as dog-meat,
I'm a horse. I can't answer back

For now, I am still in my stable,
Snow forgotten, spring gone,
Summer's here,
Last night I overheard voices,
The words instilled in me, deep fear.

Wednesday, I go to the horse-sales,
Pray for me - just an old mare
Let someone just take an interest
Let someone just want to care!

Sheila Smith

PLEASE HELP ME

Please help me, someone find me who will care.
They took me away, made me into a Dancing Bear.
They killed my mum, took and hid me away.
Now I am beaten, forced to dance - no longer play.
I'm only young, a little cub, I want my mum -
want to be loved.
Instead just pain, holes in my face with ropes that rub.
I want to be free, like the person who has done this to me.
He has his mum, lots of food, warmth at night.
Me I have nothing, no food, no love, no future in sight.
Please help me, I want to be free. To play in the grass, to rub
against a tree.
Maybe tomorrow I will be found, free of dancing, rope that
I'm bound. Someone out there, does love, does care - will
find me.
And at last others and I will have no pain but a future -
will be free.

Maureen Russell

MY BEARS

I have a large collection of bears
From all over the house they sit and stare,
Some are large and some are small
The biggest is nearly five feet tall,
From all kinds of materials they are made:
Knitted, wood, silver and jade,
Some are furry, some feel cold,
Some are young and some are old,
In fact there is such a large amount
I've never had time to sit and count.
Pictures of real bears are on walls and filed,
For their true place is in the wild.

Jan Clayton

THE TIGER

Stripes so precise,
Drawn with a ruler.
Spreading then closing again.
All mathematically worked out.

Almost as well planned as
An over-rehearsed play.
Almost as precise as
A gun shot.

Between two stripes,
Accurately measured,
Carefully placed,
Kept quiet till the last second.

> Solve that maths problem
> If it's possible.

Jessica-Ann Jenner

BROWN BEAR

Young, adorable, cuddly bear
Agonising ropes and chains you wear
Not deserving your cruel fate
Longing for freedom from those you hate.

Constantly prodded to dance yet again
Injustice and torture proceeds without end
Oh for relief from stinging blows
And a peace you have never known.

You still remember the evil day
They killed your mother then took you away
The world must learn about your plight
And protect you with all its might.

Lydia Tweed

JUST AN ANIMAL

'He's just an animal,' they said.
I felt my anger rise;
I thought of dogs who gave to me
A lifetime's love and friendship free.
Such faithfulness we like to see
Within a close-knit family.
I thought of timid sheep and cattle,
Noble horses killed in battle
Gentle donkeys, hunted hares
Tiny squirrels, dancing bears.
Comparisons are odious - yes,
That is a well-known creed.
For action vile and lustful deed
They said he was an animal;
I knew he was a man.

D Sutton

BEARS

Where have all the bears gone
I know not
Never to roam with their young.
Now their freedom has gone
Lost forever in a world of darkness.
The mother I see crying out for her young
If only she knew her young are dead.
I hear her cries call out to me
But I know that she too will soon be dead,
You poor helpless bear
How I cry for you.

Mary Welsh

The Awakening

A dainty velvet paw with the touch of thistledown
Lightly moves across my face, I twitch and sigh and frown.
A feeble ray of sunlight sneaks through the windowpane
And gentle eyes peer down at me, as sleep I try to feign.
My body feels so warm and snug, I want to sleep some more.
But there it goes, once again, that damned insistent paw.

Fond memories of my mother when waking me for school.
She would always pat my face, as a general rule.
Her soft blue eyes would smile at me, warm fingers touch my head.
You naughty little lazy-bones, you must get out of bed.
A golden pair of loving eyes now beam down at me.
Together with a rumbling purr, they state a similar plea.

I yawn and stretch and smile at her, my lovely Daisy cat.
The gentle head that nuzzles me receives a loving pat.
Where are the greys I say to her and give a little call.
Two silver shadows saunter softly down the hall.
Emerald eyes still sleepy, gaze with welcome into mine
And I know by all that's certain my day will turn out fine.

Annette Lloyd

Bears

Hip hip hooray for Libearty
They do the best they can
To help and save the bears we love
I really am a fan.

To see a bear that dances
Is a horrific sight.
And knowing how they suffer
Please give thought to their plight.

And bears kept in small cages
Their gall bladders being tapped
It breaks my heart to see them
Oh why are they so trapped?

I'd like to say a Thank you
To all of you that care.
The many supporters of Libearty
That help to save the bear.

Wendy Marchant

FORGOTTEN

Forgotten is the only word I can think of to describe,
the horrible abused feeling that I try to put aside.
I think of all the good things that maybe I could have done,
but as I look upon my past there is not even one.
I have no food, I have no drink,
I find it very hard to think.
All I have to live on is a muddy patch of grass,
that hardly any people or vehicles ever pass.
If I have not already told you
I used to be a wonderful grey,
but now in this muddy old field
I look like a dirty old bay.
All I can do is stand and stare,
All I can think is it's not fair.
I think of all those horses with the wonderful lives they run,
with all that play and all that fun their lives have just begun.
My ribs stick out, my skin sinks in,
I know I'm getting very thin.
Over the years my hope grows rotten,
I've lived no life, I was just forgotten.

Rachel Linden

EXPLOITATION

For this bear's bile,
worth thirteen times the price of gold
the Chinese will defile
with torture, and withhold
its joyful Liberty: This deprivation,
to gratify oriental aspiration.

They do not love the bear,
Nor value it in it's own right.
Neither do they care
that westerners denounce it's frightful plight.
Bewildered, terrified, in pain,
how can the bear complain
against such ignorance and greed.
Tell me please, will no-one intercede?

Kit Jackson

THE LION

An old lion in the cage on the right,
Rests his tired head on his paws,
And dreams of his days of freedom,
Oh to be free again,
To run through the grass and feel the wind on his face once more,
To watch cubs splash in the water,
To bask in the heat of the African sun,
He longs for the things he should have had but were snatched from him,
As he was snatched from his mother's side,
To live here, to be stared at,
It's not so clear now. This is home, the only home.
Home for eternity.

Jennifer Thomson

EVERY DAY COULD BE ITS LAST

Every day could be its last,
The day of the bear could be in the past,
Only a memory for me to share,
A picture on the wall at which I stare,
I see it coming, I know its fate,
But cannot stop it, it may be too late.

All it needs is a bang of a gun,
And down will fall yet another one,
In my mind I have no doubt,
The bear's life-span could run out,
It now can run wild and free
But tomorrow who knows? Not me.

I feel it is so out of place,
To centre this earth around our race,
It could be the end of a precious life,
And at only one slash of a human's knife,
Is this all in God's plan?
To have a world full up with man?

To kill a big wild strong bear,
Can't you see it's just not fair?
Every day could be its last,
The weeks are numbered, they go so fast,
Before you know, there will be no more,
Without them, to me, the world will seem poor.

I must help now, before it's too late,
Don't put if off to another date,
Soon all that this world will be,
Is one full of humans like you and me,
The only thing that's left to say,
Is I hope I never see that day.

Claire Capp

SWAN

On lakes or rivers is often seen
a creature so regal like a queen,
its presence will always delight
for the swan is a majestic sight.

Every swan is graceful in motion
and seldom displays any emotion,
but danger it will bravely face
when protecting its chosen place.

A swan has charm and much appeal
and affection for a mate is real,
swans may stay together for life
without bouts of pique or strife.

Despite their size swans can fly
and rise with power into the sky,
over fields and water they glide
escorting their mates with pride.

Together swans build a huge nest
and defend it against every pest,
later when lively cygnets appear
the proud parents stay ever near.

Stately swans are white or black
and friends they will never lack,
may these birds noble from birth
long continue to grace the Earth.

David Rigby

THE CAT CULL

They searched us out from high and low
Cats and kittens - all had to go,
I shivered in a stranger's hand
To die or live - his to command.

He took me home my eyes shut tight
I was so small, so full of fright,
A tiny breath could blow away
My little life - that dreadful day.

Between my jaws a trickle ran
Of warm sweet milk from that safe hand,
Opened my eyes to light and sun
For life was mine - and life was fun.

You are my mum - you are my dad,
When you are near my heart is glad.
My purr is full of ecstasy
I can't forget you rescued me.

Out of a world of dark and fear,
Into a world of warmth and cheer.
Now you need me - here I am
'Cos I've been there - I understand.

I cannot chase the clouds away
Or help you through the darkest day.
But I can crawl on to your knee,
Your 'Lucky' - in adversity.

C Steele

SET THEM FREE

Animals, I love you, you steal my heart, my life -
Animals, I love you; oh! to save you all from strife.
The suffering endured - at the hands of us - mankind -
cannot be imagined - the torment of your minds
We cripple and we torture you,
for want and human greed -
We keep you chained in pens, just to meet our needs.
We savage and abuse you - solely for our naked gain,
And really don't imagine that you even feel the pain.
Your eyes are purely trusting,
Even though we smite again -
You still will never fail us, will return to us in vain.
And we will smite a second time
To kill or just to maim -
Without a thought of thy pure love
A sight that still remains.
Oh Lord, if I could give my life -
This I would gladly do -
To end their pain and suffering,
That they may return to you.
I never could imagine that Jesus died for me -
But now I know the very truth -
I'd die to set them free.

Ella Meah

UNTITLED

Why is this such a cruel world,
One full of pain and grief ? -
For most of Earth's inhabitants
There's often no relief.

Four-legged ones, so much endure,
They are the victims often
Of others, walking on two legs,
I can't describe as human.

Let's do our best to ease the pain
Of creatures, great or small;
Stop this inhuman cruelty,
Make a better world for all.

One day our task will be complete,
All cruelty then will cease,
And every creature here on Earth
Will live its life in peace.

Francis Hodgkinson

AM I A BEAR?

As I appear
And when I cuddle up near you
It's clear
The koala is a bear
Endangered in its homeland
Exported to Japan
For spectacle and amusement
Is it fair
And would you dare tell them so
Or do you care

My staple diet is eucalyptus leaves
I roam the trees in an endless search for these
'But I am not a bear'!
But you appear
And when you cuddle up near me
It's clear
That this bear may be in the future
So rare
You will regretfully
Shed a tear.

John Curtis Maddison

THE DANCING BEAR

His legs were beaten
To make him stand,
His nose was pierced,
To make him suffer,
He was chained to a wall,
Eighteen hours a day,
And given no water for all that time,
Just a small piece of stale bread.

But that young bear,
He didn't give up,
He had faith.
He trusted us
To set him free,
And stop his pain.

So when we arrived,
His little heart was filled with joy,
He let us take care of him,
He let us take him home,
For he believed in us,
He believed that we would never leave him on his own.

Lindsey Maggs

AN APPEAL TO GOD

Let the turtle lay its eggs,
Let the bear keep its legs,
Let the eagle fly on high
Without a bullet in its eye.

Let the monkey live in the tree,
Let the whale swim in the sea,
Let the tiger be free to roam
In the jungle, in its home.

But:
Lock the people in a cage,
Whatever their sex, whatever their age,
Make the world a safer place
For every other living race.

Alistair Bain

GUILT

How cold you must feel lying in a rain drenched field
Lonely apart from your own
It's cold now, as you sense
Your young huddle around your body
The warmth, their only security.

Soon in the darkness, they will come
And separate mother from her young.

With terror in your eyes
Then you hear their cries
Humans, show no feelings either way
The price on your child is already made.

You will shortly feel their pain
Spill your tears
Here their screams
Feel their terror.

Your day will come, mother
You are old now, instead of pasture
No green field for you, House of Slaughter
Mother you too, have to die
They have milked you dry
Such is mankind's greed, you are their need.

Gerry O'Neil

ANIMALS ON FILM

What will all the over-aggressive,
bloodthirsty humans do when there are
no other species left to maim and kill?
After all, you can commit crimes of
murder and genocide against
all other species with virtual impunity,
for are we not the 'Lords of Creation'
by virtue of the bullet, blade, and bow?
Perhaps when the last 'other creature'
is dead, our blood-lust will turn
its ugly head wholly upon itself,
and we, the soft caring types
will have to run for our lives
to cater for their sport, and our
death cries of terror and anguish
will be caught on film to be shown
on TV on Sunday afternoons,
thoughtfully just before
'The Antiques Roadshow'.

Philip L Fletcher

DANCING TILL DEATH

The dancing bears
At work all day
Never free to roam and play

Dancing in the searing sun
Their youth cut short
Deprived of fun

Stolen at birth
Used so cruelly
Magnificent animals treated unduly

Helen Elizabeth Rawlinson

THE CROCODILE

Primordial giant of a by-gone age,
Sculptured in sepulchral stone,
Motionless, poised, the eye of death,
A would be torturer lurking in the depths.
Jagged teeth to cut and sear.
Knuckled skin, an armoured adversary.
What malevolent thoughts pass through your brain,
Do you think beyond your next meal?
Of what pain you can inflict.
You pool glints with algae, aquatic camouflage
Hides your notorious smile.
Yet the alter ego.
A giant mother with infinitesimal care,
Nurtures her eggs.
The gentle squeaks as babe after babe is ferried to safety,
In gaping jaws.
Oh misunderstood monster, we live in
Fear of your threat.
But how great you are.
Caught between the two kingdoms of hate and respect.

Carol Lycett

FREEDOM

Running through the valley or trees
Light piercing through the leaves
Like phantom shadows on the ground
You bob and weave as the trees sway around
Like a child at play, the world is with you all the way
Diving in pools and catching fish
Salmon is a tasty dish
Playing in the wilderness, this is your domain

So let's work together to keep the wilderness and the brown bear.

Jim Deakin

ANIMAL POEM

Bears like all animals should be safe from harm
not in cages held with chains,
or foxes hunted by huntsmen running to their fate.

Badgers seem so tame and domestic yet
human beings still bait them in their sets.

Animal testing, I can't help but wonder
how these poor animals cope
torn from families scared and confused
writing to MP's gives us a little hope.

Whales and dolphins are creatures of the sea,
beautiful, graceful and with elegancy.

But man still persist to harpoon and trap in nets
which is so damn cruel and callous it makes you vexed.

Fur trade how horrible does that sound,
if only we could have that banned, turned around.

The stoat, mink, silver fox, and rabbit
would love a fur free life, so make it a habit.

When it comes to bull fighting there's nothing to say
but matadors will pay when the bull has its day.

Andrea Sidney

PROTECT OUR ANIMALS

Though man may be the master
Of all creatures great and small
He has a duty to protect them
For our children one and all.
To kill these lovely creatures
Causes suffering and pain,
Some people call it pleasure
Others do it just for gain.

They were created just like us
To enjoy this world of ours,
And we must not destroy them
Just because we have the powers.
To continue their destruction
Man will have to bear the cost,
So let's live with them in harmony
Before they too are lost.

Kenneth J Ody

MERCY ON MONTSERRAT

They fled and left me all alone
Here in the volcano zone.
Abandoned me to living hell,
Those people I had loved so well.

Eyes blinded by the ash
Sniffing for food in piles of trash.
'Tis day or night I cannot tell,
Bright sun shrouded by a veil.

Fumes and heat rise from the ground,
While all the time that roaring sound.
Un-ending time, great despair,
Made manifest, a dark nightmare.

But wait a minute, joy of joys,
Can it be a human's voice?
More than one, quite a few,
Then the forms come into view.

Ecstasy! I rush to greet
Forgetting my poor blistered feet.
Loving friends, can it be?
Oh yes, they've come to rescue me!

Marjorie Houston

BROWN EYES

Look into my eyes, what do you see
Pain, sorrow, sadness, hopelessness
I'm chained, shackled made to perform
To dance, to entertain the tourists.

Looking out of my eyes, what do I see
My master keeping hold of my chains
My home such as it is, a refuse spot
The tourists uncertain what to do.

Look into my eyes, what do you see
A glimmer, a faint spark of hope
I'm in a sanctuary now, being cared for
I can forage, bathe, eat proper bear food.

Looking out of my eyes, what do I see
Helpful, kind, friendly people smiling
Green grass, trees, water
Other bears just like me, lived my life.

Look into my eyes, what do you see
Warmth, happiness, contentment, freedom
I'm in the wilderness now, free
I can fish, forage, do as I please.

Looking out of my eyes, what do I see
Streams, rivers, mountains, woods
Other bears, some babies, free, wild
I see my home where I belong.

Thank you Libearty, you gave me
What is rightfully mine
My freedom to be a wild bear
My eyes tell that story.

Carol Deakin

LYNX IN THE SNOW

        First the eyes -
Rise on tiptoe, slow . . .
Stop. Glow
Of recognition riveted
To the hare.
Listen to its jumping,
Whirling, chukkering - all different.
        Today, earth crackles.
Water creaks and hardens.
Fur-flurries from bruised sky fly
Into and round the
Widened eyes.
        There. Stare
At throat raised, sensing air,
Struggling, before the event,
To breathe what now is rare -
and frozen. All -
Hare, lynx, earth and the moment, till,
(Surprise of such hot blood
In recent frost of denser hair),
From ice-still, *there* -
A dash, a flash, a gash,
No time for prayer.

        And when I go,
Enormous footprints in the snow.

Marie Hurlston

Fighting Bear

I am but a humble, beautiful bear,
For life so cruel, I do not care.
They come, they stare, they jeer and gloat,
At my sunken eyes and lack lustre coat.

I live to fight another day.
May this be the last I sometimes pray.
Snatched from my mother at tender age,
To be kept in starvation in a rancid cage.

My brothers fight, my sisters dance,
Dare I take a second glance.
Another brother is ripped to pieces,
Only on death, all anguish ceases.

Please God will someone help my plight,
So that I may be spared the fight.
I've done no wrong, I've done no harm,
My life could have been so full of charm.

The handlers come, I'm dragged out once more,
To ban this maltreatment, there should be a law.
I am but a humble, beautiful bear,
If death comes now, what do I care.

Lyn Errington

When The Cruelty Stops

When animals don't have to suffer,
from people indifferent to their cries,
who in the name of greed and sport,
inflict pain seen in glazed eyes
when will the cruelty stop?
We must try to make them understand
this world is not just ours

animals do have a rightful place on earth.
Like moon and stars and flowers,
oh for a change of attitude.
When compassion comes to stay
and all animals treated with humanity
will we ever see that day?
When the cruelty stops.

P E Tidswell

CHIMP

Blank faces and saddened eyes,
Your freedom has been denied.

Show me warmth in a cold man's world,
Show me a clenched fist, unfurled.
You thirst for love and a tender hand,
Your wish is lost in this senseless land.
Bound by chains and human minds -
This, the threat, is called mankind.
Teased and tormented all the while,
You will escape in the course of time.

So climb into your world of dreams,
Away from reality and hidden fears;
Draw up strength from the depths of your heart;
Wait for the day to make a new start.
And I will think of you as time passes by,
And wish and hope this end is nigh.

Blank faces and saddened eyes,
Your soul lives on, you will never die.

Tania Sutlieff

Sunday Morning . . .

Sunday morning outings upon horse back,
Immaculate dress and all that.
Guffaws of laughter and merriment.
Though conversations can turn serious like 'how the cricket went'
'Oh life is so jolly for our breed.'
Kept intact through generations of greed.
Jealously like the pastures we own is green,
Wanting our privileges that their eyes have seen,
Like this meeting here today
For only we can legally behave this way,
It's a tradition that we have made our own
For we pass the laws with which you've grown.
When will you accept life is made for our kind?
Far superior in body, wallet and mind
And most important, no matter what the cost
You'll never get back what you don't know you've even lost!
Life is for laughing at fools who try
To expose the truth which for us is so easy to deny
Anyway enough of this idle chatter
One must dash back to the relevant matter
For our pack of privilege must seek out and destroy
Nature's nasty creatures that do so annoy
So much so that our hounds deserve such exercise
Like reducing vermin to nothing before our very eyes
So tally ho master, saddle up and sound your horn
See, so sporting are we, the prey we'll even warn!
So really, there's no excuse to get caught
Which is our justified excuse to call this murder, a sport.

David Hardy

THE PRISONER

I'm tired!
It's such an effort to move.
My paws are weighted down.
My heart is with my paws.

Even if I had freedom
Even if I wasn't chained
I have no where to move to.
I'm restricted by a metal frame.
Don't know who put it there.
Wish they'd take it away;
I'm scared!

Sometimes they make me exercise.
I don't have a choice.
Resistance is too painful.
If I don't move my face hurts
And burns and stings.
Why do they do it?

It's hard to accept
That everyone lives like this.
Or is it just existence?
I become surrounded and panic,
Try to escape but there's no hope.
I'm constantly taunted and tortured
Defenceless against their power.

I'm tired!
My paws ache
My head throbs.
I'm lonely, frightened, confused.

Just let me rest . . . Please!

Rachel Martin

THE BEAR'S PRAYER

Oh God of bears to you I pray
Help me through this long, long day.
The rifle's bullet loud and clear
Started me on this life of fear.
My mother lay dead, how could I know
That never again through the woods I'd go?
And thus my life of shame began
I was taught to walk like man.
I suffer fire, the stick the rope,
I live a life bereft of hope.
A cage at night is now my home
No more the liberty to roam.
But if at any time I'm freed
No longer the object of my owner's greed,
Then God of bears to you I'll pray
Help my brothers through their day.

Jenny Prin

SO YOUNG

Don't you know, it's oh so wrong
To make a bear dance to a song
Can't you see his look of anguish,
his captors to hell, should be banished.
To make him dance, and perform,
a hole in his pallet must be bore.
A piece of rope is threaded through,
his screams of pain would deafen you.
His life of hell has just begun
it breaks my heart in one so young.
13 hours in searing heat
Made to dance on India's streets.

Carol Bones

THE VIXEN

I share my garden,
At night
And feed on love of beauty as
She feeds on scraps I've strewn her way.
No cub, but young
My guest
The vixen fox
Whose paws trip over grass I've mown
And dig the soil wherein I've planted seeds.
Though none will grow as she
Or move with her dexterity of dignity

Lively is her want
Her red ears pricked.
I hardly dare to breathe
In case she thinks to fear me.
Then she goes. Too soon
And I am left
Alone to own my garden
And my dreams, of snow -
Then I'd see her footprints
Then I'd be not left so utterly bereft.
O come tomorrow
Vixen fox
Come and share the moon by which I see you gracile in my garden.
Come
Come soon.

Lynne Chitty

Innocent Victim

It was inevitable
But should not have been,
Watching him, writhing on the table
In that sterile room,
So far removed from his ideal
I cried, inside.

Rescued, early from a 'gun obsessed'
Tammy accepted me,
Twin brother of that wraith-like shadow
They grew strong together.

I watched, saddened, knowing.
Insidious extermination of a perfect creature
Victim of man's abysmal greed
And ignorance,
Brave, trusting, patient.
Day by day he waited
Always there - never straying.

His companions knew,
I watched them too.
They comforted, washed and fed him
Food they'd caught.

I brought him back
All life spent
And piteously his sister cried,
Keening round the carry box.

In the garden he lies now
In his favourite spot.
Where summer sun shone warmly
On silken fur:
Side by side with two
Other faithful friends.
I miss him.

Helen Perry

UNTITLED

The early Christians, so they say,
Were thrown for savage beasts to slay:
In the arena, Caesar's crowd
For gory pleasure roared aloud.

And still today this sport is shown.
But beasts are now to Christians thrown!
The bullfight is an odd reverse,
And to my mind it's even worse.

The same harsh pit; the same coarse cheers,
We could be back two-thousand years:
Is this all Christians can achieve?
Then give me beasts, and Man . . . I'll leave!

C P Goodwin

ANIMALS

Will you come with me to the zoo?
You'll see lots of animals here are a few,
Chimpanzees cheekily swing in their cage,
Elephants live to a wonderful age,
Polar bears dive and play in their pool,
In the heat of summer they like to keep cool,
Giraffes stretch their necks, oh they are tall,
Is that a sea lion playing with a ball?
Cuddly pandas chew bamboo shoots,
An enormous rhino digs at some roots,
A sleepy lion lolls in the sun,
Do come with me, we can have fun.

Veronica Searle

INFORMATION

We hope you have enjoyed reading this book - and that you will continue to enjoy it in the coming years.

If you like reading and writing poetry drop us a line, or give us a call, and we'll send you a free information pack.

Write to :-
 **Poetry Now Information
 1-2 Wainman Road
 Woodston
 Peterborough
 PE2 7BU
 (01733) 230746**